THE POWER OF
POLARITIES

AN INNOVATIVE METHOD TO TRANSFORM
INDIVIDUALS, TEAMS, AND ORGANIZATIONS.
BASED ON CARL JUNG'S THEORY OF
THE PERSONALITY.

BY

JOHN VAN DER STEUR

"*The Power of Polarities* is a lively and serious contribution to the literature on Jung's psychological types theory and its practical application. The emphasis on polarities is fundamental and salutary."

~ **Dr. Murray Stein, PhD**, Jungian Analyst, Author, and former President of the International Association for Analytical Psychology (IAAP) and the International School of Analytical Psychology (ISAP).

THE POWER
—— OF ——
POLARITIES

AN INNOVATIVE METHOD TO TRANSFORM
INDIVIDUALS, TEAMS, AND ORGANIZATIONS.
BASED ON CARL JUNG'S THEORY OF
THE PERSONALITY.

BY
JOHN VAN DER STEUR

www.powerofpolarities.com
www.polarityconsulting.com

Copyright © 2018 John van der Steur

All rights reserved. No reproduction, transmission or copy of this publication can be made in any form without the written consent of the author, except as permitted by United States Copyright Law.

Published by Polarity Institute, Austin, Texas.
The Power of Polarities is a registered trademark (Reg. U.S. Pat. & Tm. Off.).
www.powerofpolarities.com

First Edition, 2017

ISBN: 978-0-9993253-0-8

Library of Congress Catalog Number - 2017962825
Polarity Institute, Austin, TX

Although the author and publisher have made every effort to ensure that the information provided in this publication is correct, the author and publisher do not assume and hereby disclaim any liability to any party for any loss, damage, or disruption caused by errors, omissions or contrary interpretation of the subject matter herein, whether such errors, omissions or contrary interpretation of the subject matter herein result from negligence, accident, or any other cause.

Adherence to all applicable laws and regulations, including international, federal, state, and local governing professional licensing, business practices, advertising, and all other aspects of doing business in the US, Canada or any other jurisdiction is the sole responsibility of the reader and consumer. Neither the author nor the publisher assumes any responsibility or liability whatsoever on behalf of the consumer or reader of this material.

The views expressed in this publication are those of the author alone and are strictly for educational purposes. They should not be used to replace the specialized training and professional judgment of a mental health care professional.

Neither the author nor the publisher can be held responsible for the use of the information provided within this publication. Please always consult a trained professional before making any decision regarding treatment of yourself or others.

This publication contains copyrighted material the use of which has not always been specifically authorized by the copyright owner. The author and publisher believe this constitutes 'fair use' as provided for in section 107 of the US Copyright Law and serves a strictly educational purpose.

The use of trademarks and brands within this publication is for clarification only and without prior consent from their owners.

The author reserves the right to make any changes he deems necessary for the sake of accuracy to future versions of this publication.

Publishing Services provided by Happy Self Publishing.
www.happyselfpublishing.com
Author photograph by Pieter van der Steur.

Free Bonus Materials
Get Your Personality Profile and Workbook
https://www.powerofpolarities.com/bonusmaterials

To my daughters, Eline and Mea.
I love you with all my heart and am proud to be your father.
Every day I learn more from you than I could ever teach you.
May your curiosity, innocence, and excitement lead you to find your pearl
in life.

On Children

Your children are not your children.
They are the sons and daughters of Life's longing for itself.
They come through you but not from you,
And though they are with you, yet they belong not to you.

You may give them your love but not your thoughts.
For they have their own thoughts.
You may house their bodies but not their souls,
For their souls dwell in the house of tomorrow,
which you cannot visit, not even in your dreams.
You may strive to be like them, but seek not to make them like you.
For life goes not backward nor tarries with yesterday.

You are the bows from which your children as living arrows are sent
forth.
The archer sees the mark upon the path of the infinite,
and He bends you with His might that His arrows may go swift and far.
Let your bending in the archer's hand be for gladness;
For even as He loves the arrow that flies,
so He loves also the bow that is stable.

~ Kahlil Gibran

Foreword

It has been said of C.G. Jung, that he didn't want disciples sitting at his feet, but colleagues standing on his shoulders. John van der Steur has his feet firmly planted on the shoulders of this patriarch of modern psychology, C.G. Jung.

The author uses Jung's theory of psychological types as a launching device for understanding the personal and collective psyche. He wisely discerns that the theory of opposites, or the facts of life's polarities, hold many resources for the expansion of consciousness, decision making, self-understanding, and healthy relationships.

The integration of opposites is a necessary conscious pursuit in order to find a balanced mental health. The "non-dual" mind is able to find meaning in holding the tension between polar opposites. It knows this leads to necessary transformation and higher consciousness. Such practice can arrive at the wisdom of understanding that the worst thing that ever happened to me was also the best thing that ever happened to me.

The major contribution John van der Steur's interpretation of Jung's typology is that it expands, innovates and explains the dynamic of psychological types. Further, in this study, one receives an excellent summary of the history of Jung's thought in his school of analytical psychology. From historical references to personal anecdote, the author makes complicated material very understandable. His approach to polarities has the potential to function as an antidote to the poison of division and polarization in society today. In that sense this book is very timely.

This book is a valuable study and an excellent resource for understanding the human personality, but more importantly, a resource for understanding oneself.

J. Pittman McGehee
Austin, Texas, 2017.

J. Pittman McGehee, INFP, is a Jungian analyst and Episcopal priest in private practice in Austin, Texas. He is widely known as a lecturer and educator in the field of psychology and religion, as well as a published poet and essayist. He is the author of *The Invisible Church: Finding Spirituality Where You Are*, *Raising Lazarus: The Science of Healing the Soul*, *Words Made Flesh*, and *The Paradox of Love*. In college, he played Forward on the 1966 Oklahoma State Cowboys basketball team.

Table of Contents

Foreword ix

Introduction 1

Chapter 1: The Illusion of Power 9

Chapter 2: The Purpose of Polarities 17

Chapter 3: Towards a More Conscious Ego 35

Chapter 4: Shoulders to Stand On 45

Chapter 5: The Purpose of Jungian Psychology 55

Chapter 6: Jungian Typology 101 67

Chapter 7: The Inferior Function: A Blessing in Disguise 91

Chapter 8: Thinking and Feeling: The Great Divide 105

Chapter 9: Falsification of Type: The Problem of the Great Pretender 117

Chapter 10: The Typological Octahedron 127

Chapter 11: Temperament, Type, and Color 145

Chapter 12: The Power of Purpose 159

Chapter 13: Teamology - The Power of Polarities in Practice 175

Epilogue 195

Appendix I: Symbol of the American Dream: National
Mall in Washington, D.C. 197

Appendix II: Other Interpretations of Jung's Psychological
Types 205

Appendix III: 1995 Interview with Robert A. Johnson 217

Bibliography 231

Disclaimer 237

Acknowledgements 239

About the Author 241

To side with either of these two great realities—heaven and earth—is an error. Over time I came to appreciate that a middle place in which both realms are honored is not only the safest place, it also is the ecstatic place, the holy place. If one works faithfully and patiently at this task of balancing heaven and earth, eventually one may even realize something more remarkable: that the two worlds are in fact one.

~ Robert A. Johnson and Jerry Ruhl, Balancing Heaven and Earth, 2009, Prologue

The psyche is the greatest of all cosmic wonders and the "sine qua non" of the world as we know it. It is in the highest degree odd that Western man, with but very few exceptions, pays so little regard to this fact.

~ Carl Jung, Structure & Dynamics of the Psyche, 1969, § 357

Health and growth are not optional in the psychological sphere, any more than they are in the physical.

~ Murray Stein, The Principle of Individuation, 2006, p. 5

The surest way to corrupt a youth is to instruct him to hold in higher esteem those who think alike than those who think differently.

~ Friedrich Nietzsche, The Dawn of Day, 1881, Sec. 297

Every man has a vocation to be someone: but he must understand clearly that, in order to fulfill his vocation, he can only be one person: himself.

~ Thomas Merton, No Man Is an Island, 1955.

Not nature, but the "genius of mankind," has knotted the hangman's noose with which it can execute itself at any moment.

~ Carl Jung, Psychology and Religion: West and East, 1970, § 734

Introduction

There is a vitality, a life force, an energy, a quickening that is translated through you into action, and because there is only one of you in all of time, this expression is unique. People have asked me why I chose to be a dancer. I did not choose: I was chosen to be a dancer, and with that, you live all your life.

~ Martha Graham, modern dancer and choreographer

Polarities are real, and they are everywhere. Light-Dark, Ebb-Flow, High-Low, In-Out, Rest-Movement, Hot-Cold. When the poles within a polarity are in balance, there is life and growth, but if there is imbalance the system self-destructs. This is not only a physical truth; it is a psychological truth as well. And it is the driving force behind some of the greatest human achievements, as well as catastrophes.

I have often asked myself what explains the impact we have, whether as an individual, team, or organization. Why, for instance, is the average lifespan of companies listed on the stock exchange a mere eighteen years? Why is it that Olympic "favorites" often fail? What makes talented young adults get stuck and miss fulfilling their potential or sometimes simply self-destruct? How is it possible that a "little general" like Napoleon created a vast European empire and lost it all within fifteen years?

On the brighter side of human achievement, what explains the phenomenal success of Apple? How could John Wooden win ten national titles in twelve years as head basketball coach at UCLA? How could the Beatles have such a profound impact as "The Fab Four," but never reach those heights individually? Or—and this is one of my personal favorites—how did Dutch soccer player and coach Johan Cruyff motivate his teams to win championships as consistently as he did? As a player, he won the European Champions League three times in a row. As a coach, he propelled FC Barcelona (currently considered one of the world's best teams) to its first ever Champions League victory in 1992, but more importantly he created a high performing culture that lasts until today.

As an economist, management consultant, entrepreneur, facilitator of team processes, and in my own intrapersonal work, I discovered a pattern that I call "the power of polarities." This power has the capability to either destroy or energize the whole. It can drive individuals, teams, and organizations to either underperform or attain unusually high levels of performance.

I never saw this more clearly than in the work I did with sports teams, specifically in the work I did with the Dutch women's field hockey team in the two years preceding the 2012 London Olympics where they won the gold medal. This team was talented, but in sports it usually is not the best players that win a championship, it is the best team. A group of players that does not function as a team tends to fall apart under pressure. This is what happened with this team during some of their matches. Their coach asked me to help him build a strong, unified whole from the very disparate personalities within the team, a team that could win at the moment of truth. I knew nothing of field hockey as a sport, so I had an unbiased perspective and a particularly fruitful advantage: I could focus solely on their team processes with no historical perspective or personal investment to distract me.

After teaching the team and staff members to understand their individual and each other's personality types, we worked on defining a shared purpose. We spent a few sessions mapping this out and installing it firmly into consciousness. Individual players were given roles that suited their personality. As a result, less prominent players on the team began making important contributions based on the knowledge they had gained about their unique capabilities and corresponding personality type. Slowly, a unified team began to emerge that was more in balance and could handle the pressure of the semi-finals and finals at the Olympics. The pressure became an agent for positive change for this team, and they used it well.

When the polarities in a team harmonize, their power energizes the whole, and extraordinary human achievements become possible. This is what I like to call the *Power of Polarities*, and I have seen this dynamic repeatedly with the teams I have worked with, but never more clearly than with the Dutch women's hockey team. Their teamwork harmonized the polarities in the team, and it earned them a gold medal at the 2012 London Olympics. Their motto? *"Teamwork Makes the Dream Work."*

I learned more from this field hockey team than I taught them. They and the other teams with which I have worked have not only shown me the miracle of human achievement, but also the practical steps that lead to high performance. The advantage of working with a sports team is that the results are tangible and straightforward. Sports teams get concrete feedback every game they play because they either win or lose.

There is a principle at work here that I call the "four-legged table." When one leg of this table is missing, it can remain standing but collapses under pressure. But a table with four legs is rock solid, even when a lot of weight or pressure is applied to it. Whether as an individual or as part of a team or an organization, we have likely all experienced this in one way or another. We develop a narrow view, overlook something, and topple over under pressure.

Think for a moment of a child learning how to bike. It is not until a child can balance on the bike that he or she graduates from a tricycle to a bicycle. Life is not kind to lopsidedness, but it is to balance. There is one critical ingredient that we need as individuals, teams, and organizations to overcome one-sidedness: purpose. Purpose is like the solid tabletop that holds the four legs of the table together. If a purpose is powerful enough, the whole personality of the individual or team will rally behind it, make the necessary sacrifices, and endure the hardships to "make the dream work."

The "four-legged table" that I help individuals, teams and organizations is based on the personality theory of the Swiss psychologist Carl Jung. His "typology" is a mental model not only for solving problems, but for great human achievement. As a psychologist, Jung had a unique ability to reason in terms of polarities. For example, conscious-unconscious, introvert-extravert, ego-shadow, masculine-feminine, heart-mind, sadness-joy, and so on. And his typology is based on the polarities in the personality. Typology in this context refers to the study, mapping, and understanding of our personality "types." This process helps to see ourselves in a new light, revealing the dichotomous or dual aspects of our personalities. These polarities are like opposite sides of the same coin, and we all have and use both, whether we are aware of it or not. At the same time, we all have natural, inborn talents that are important to acknowledge and use.

One of the great paradoxes of life is that the purpose of polarities is not to polarize but to harmonize. Within a polarity, one pole cannot exist without the other. They are in fact intended to work together. The ability to access both sides of the equation, the plus, and the minus, is where the great challenge for human consciousness lies. As a species, our consciousness is our most important, most powerful and at the same time most under-utilized resource. Jung set out to change this.

When Jung published his work *Psychological Types* in 1921, it was considered a revelation. A 1923 New York Times review of the English translation states: *"He (Jung) has shown that each person has a right to live according to his own type, and his presentation of the guiding principles for the recognition of the type is one of the most humanitarian achievements that has become manifest... This volume is drastically serious, positive, didactic, classic and yet more than stimulating. It is energizing, liberating and recreative... The author shows an amazingly sympathetic and comprehensive knowledge of the introvert of the Thinking type, and hardly less of his other types."*

Since 1921 Jung's work has found its practical application in many personality instruments. Of these the Myers-Briggs Type Indicator® or MBTI® is the most well-known. This instrument was developed by a mother (Katherine Briggs) and daughter (Isabel Myers) in the 1940's and is the most widely used personality type indicator today. This mother-and-daughter team deserves credit for the popularization of and research into Jung's typology by educating tens of millions of people all over the planet on their personality type.

The polarities in the personality run deep and go beyond gender, race, culture, or religion. When we consider another person—like our opposite in terms of type—we might think, *"I can't believe you would think this way! I don't get it, are you crazy? Are you being difficult on purpose?"* Yet, different types are often interdependent and, when connected, always create something unusually valuable, something they could not have created independently

Our personality is a psychological reality just like our body is a physical reality. We are aware of how our body functions: when we walk we put one foot in front of the other. But are we also aware of how our personality functions and how we can best use it? Whatever roles one has in life, the personality provides one with unique capabilities to use in those roles.

The Power of Polarities is a book based on 30 years of experience with Jung, personality types and purpose gained while working with individuals, teams, and organizations. It attempts to view Jung's work on typology in a new light, aided by almost a century of experience with its practical application. It also attempts to support it with a broader foundation than type alone. Other concepts in Jungian psychology such as the role of consciousness, the ego, the Shadow, and personal purpose are interconnected with type and are essential to consider when talking about type.

There was a moment in my life that I discovered that my purpose in this life is to help people discover the truths that sustain them, the truths that give them life and vitality. In the search for truths that give me life, the work of Carl Jung has been indispensable. I came across it in my early twenties when I was an economics student at the University of Amsterdam. On some weekends, I would visit my parents in nearby The Hague. During one of those visits, my mother played cassette tapes of a Jungian seminar she was enrolled in. For some strange reason, I was immediately drawn to the content of these recordings. I could not stop listening, so I decided to appropriate them.

That was the beginning of a lifelong relationship with the work of Carl Jung. The depth and relevance of his work today are enormous and you can find his quotes all over the internet and in social media. Studying his work and undergoing Jungian analysis has provided me with the truths I need in my life. It has helped me discover my passion, what I love to do. I have had the opportunity to help hundreds of teams and thousands of people in their journeys to a life with the meaning and impact they aspire to.

My interest in typology was piqued when, in 1995, I met Robert Johnson, a Jungian analyst, and popular author. As we sat on the terrace of his small apartment in Encinitas, California, overlooking the vast Pacific Ocean, he said to me: *"When I met Jung he told me to be true to myself, and true to my type. And that is what I wish for you. If you go against your typological makeup, you go against your grain and you will get splinters. Go with it and your life will have ease, flow and purpose."*

The Power of Polarities is a book of questions, not answers. It is designed to help you find relevant questions to ask, to help you reflect on and examine your own life, to help you discover who you are and what your relationship is to yourself and the world around you. Whether you are an individual, team, or organization, this work will help you claim your authenticity and give your unique gift to humankind.

In Chapter 1-3 you will learn about the nature of polarities and the purpose they serve. Chapter 4-6 cover basic and essential information on Jung, his psychology, and his typology. In Chapter 7-9 you will discover more about the dynamic of the personality and the problem of type falsification. Chapter 10 and 11 cover the new model I have developed using Jung's theory and are rather technical and theoretical in nature. You can skip them without missing the gist of this book. In Chapter 12 you will learn how the Power of Purpose pulls everything together and in Chapter 13 you will discover how it all comes together in developing high performance teams.

The appendices contain some interesting writings that I felt did not belong in the structure of the book itself, but are a worthwhile read. Appendix I covers an interesting analogy between the National Mall in Washington D.C. and Jung's personality types. In appendix II, you will find a comparison with the other systems based on Jungian typology and in Appendix III you will find an interview I did with the popular Jungian analyst and author Robert Johnson in

1995. He is someone that inspired me many times over and I consider myself blessed that I became acquainted with him.

A word of advice, if a chapter does not interest you because of its specific technical or theoretical nature, I urge you to move on and find what supports you and your journey. Use that which applies to you to the best of your ability and feel free to disregard what you do not need.

Since this is a book of questions, it will help you find your unique answers, your unique truths. In my experience, it is wiser to trust those who seek the truth and want to help you find yours than to trust those who claim to have found yours, theirs, and everyone else's. My sincere hope is you will find in your lifetime what you need to help you be or become who you are meant to be.

Chapter 1

The Illusion of Power

Every truth has two sides; it is as well to look at both before we commit ourselves to either.

~ Aesop, Greek storyteller, 600 B.C.

There is in our world an illusion of power. The illusion is that one pole of a polarity is better than the other. One pole is right, the other wrong. One good, the other bad. One weak, the other strong. As a result, one pole is chosen at the expense of the other. The poles become divided and as we know a house that is divided cannot stand. The influence of this illusion can be seen everywhere in society: politics, religion, business, education, gender roles, sports, ecology, and so on. It leads to lopsidedness, imbalance, and crisis. True and authentic power, the kind that is sustainable (if not indestructible), is found in a balanced dynamic between the poles of a polarity.

Polarities exist in the physical and natural realm. For example, the protons and electrons in the atom, the North and South poles of our planet and the cycle of Night and Day. In nature, these polarities are organized in a balanced and self-regulated way that produces life as we know it. All it takes for the Night-Day polarity to exist is for the earth to rotate around its own axis.

With us humans it is different, we struggle with self-regulation and balance because as a species we are endowed with consciousness and free will, which means we have to find balance ourselves. Sometimes it seems as if we are moving from crisis to crisis without a clear notion of balance or sense of equilibrium.

When I was a student of economics at the University of Amsterdam, we studied "Tulipmania," one of the first economic crises in modern society. There was in the Netherlands a brief period during the early 17th century when the prices of tulip bulbs soared and made many Dutch traders very wealthy. At one point a rare tulip bulb was purchased for twelve acres of land! At the peak of this market, everyone thought that tulip bulbs were a source of everlasting wealth. Eventually the speculative bubble burst, a crisis ensued, and a new balance was found. There have been many different types of tulipmania since. The 2008 financial crisis was a form of tulipmania, evidence that we still need more awareness of the kinds of imbalances that we as humans tend to create.

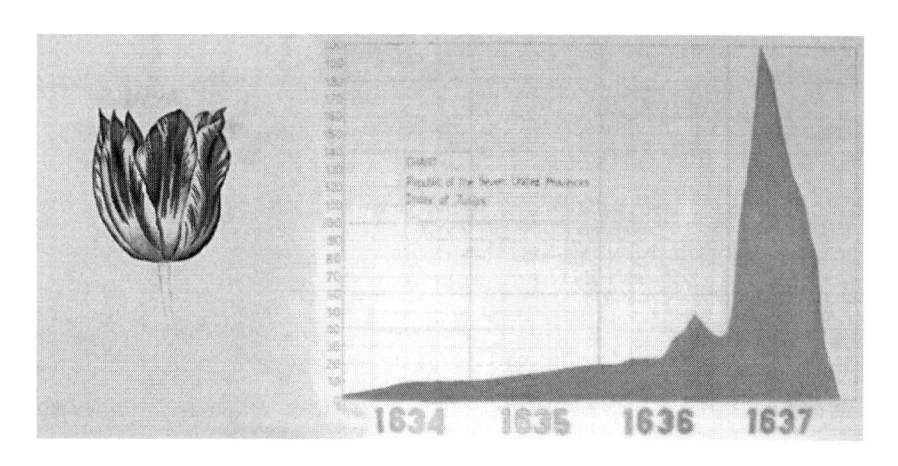

The reason we find ourselves in these types of crisis is psychological. There seems to be a distortion of reality. True power is found in balancing the poles of a polarity. But if we believe tulip bulbs are an eternal source of wealth and their prices can only rise, naturally we would invest all our savings in these bulbs and prices would continue to increase. But this is an illusion, not reality. It creates an imbalance, and there is a natural law that says every imbalance is eventually corrected to find balance. When applied to such crises, the term "crash" is very apt.

The balance and therefore the power of polarities in the human psyche depend upon our conscious choice, which is both a creative gift and a great challenge. It is how we create humanity and the human experience. We can choose our actions, but not the consequences resulting from our actions. It is not without reason that some say, "Be careful what you wish for, you might get it."

One important and unique quality in all of Jung's work is his treatment of polarities in the human psyche. In this lies the great value of his work. As far back as 600 B.C. in Ancient Greece, philosophers like Heraclitus have pondered the laws of polarities. Jung, however, had the ability to discover how polarities are constellated in the human psyche. He invented and popularized concepts like introvert-extravert, animus-anima, consciousness-unconsciousness, ego-shadow and many more. He is in fact quoted as saying, "*Something is true if the opposite is also true.*" Below are few examples that illustrate this:

Life is born only of the spark of opposites.
(Jung, CW 7, § 78)

It is the age old drama of opposites, which is fought out in every human life.
(Jung, CW 14, § 199)

In all chaos there is a cosmos, in all disorder a secret order, in all caprice a fixed law, for everything that works is grounded on its opposite.
(Jung, CW 9i, § 66)

In terms of energy, polarity means a potential, and wherever a potential exists there is the possibility of a current, a flow of events, for the tension of opposites strives for balance.
The psychological rule says that when an inner situation is not made conscious, it happens outside, as fate. That is to say, when the individual does not become conscious of his inner opposite, the world must perforce act out the conflict and be torn into opposing halves.
(Jung, CW 9ii, § 126)

Every victory contains the germ of future defeat.
(Jung, CW 9i, § 150)

Even a happy life cannot be without a measure of darkness, and the word "happy" would lose its meaning if it were not balanced by sadness.
(McGuire & Hull, 1987, p. 452)

Understanding the psyche is about understanding human consciousness, and this starts with the personality, which, as Jung explained, contains our *"functions of consciousness."*
His research into personality theory took two decades and resulted in the publication of *Psychological Types* in 1921. In the Foreword, he writes:

This book is the fruit of nearly twenty years' work in the domain of practical psychology. It grew gradually from the countless impressions and experiences of a psychiatrist in the treatment of nervous illnesses, from interaction with men and women of all social levels, from my personal dealings with friend and foe alike, and finally, from a critique of my own psychological peculiarity.

It is as important to be aware of the psychological makeup of our psyche as it is to be aware of the physical makeup of our body so that we can learn to use it and develop it. Both are essential vehicles for our participation in life. If we are not conscious of our personality, it controls us, and can sometimes lead us to places or situations we do not like. Sometimes it leads to success, but more often to failure. If we can turn this around and become of aware of our personality and take responsibility for our lives, much can be gained, and unnecessary suffering avoided.

Jung learned this from personal experience through his conflict with Sigmund Freud. In a well-known *Face-to-Face* television interview with the BBC in 1959, Jung said that he wrote his work on types for *"a very personal reason, namely to do justice to the psychology of Freud… and also to find my own bearings."* Through this work, he discovered that his and Freud's personalities were different and that their conflict was related to having different ways of viewing the world. Jung also understood that there was no right or wrong in this conflict, just contrasting views. The tragedy was that he and Freud could never integrate their points of view, primarily due to Freud's insistence on there being only one, single psychological theory and method of treatment. Jung was able to put his conflict with Freud into a different perspective through his work on personality types:

> *The book on types yielded the insight that every judgment made by an individual is conditioned by his personality type and that every point of view is necessarily relative.*
> (Jung, 1989, Chapter VII: The Work)

The critical point in this quote is *"necessarily relative."* Reality is not what is in front of the eyes, but what is behind them. And since we each have a unique pair of eyes, what you or I see with them will *necessarily* differ. Everything changes if we can accept that our point of view is relative to the observer and that there are other points of view as well. It means we always need others to arrive at a better and more complete perspective.

If we make conscious use of our whole personality, with all its internal contradictions, we can create balance in ourselves. If we remain unaware of these realities, they will lead us to unnecessarily great imbalances, crises, and suffering. What it requires is that we examine both sides of reality. What we will discover is that they are really one and that both are equally valuable. Beyond duality, there is always unity, and the purpose of polarities is to find that unity and achieve harmony. This balancing act is the great challenge of human consciousness, but also a rewarding one. In the words of Jungian analyst and author Robert A. Johnson:

If one works faithfully and patiently at this task of balancing heaven and earth, eventually one may even realize something more remarkable: that the two worlds are in fact one.
(Johnson and Ruhl, 2009, Prologue)

Perhaps this understanding is more relevant today than ever before. Many people today are experiencing a world that is divided, chaotic, polarized, and insufficiently harmonized. Nations, economies, religions, and ethnic and racial groups, amongst others, are becoming increasingly antagonistic and unbalanced. Natural law states that unbalanced polarities are unstable and will eventually self-destruct. Therefore, it pays to be mindful of how polarization can become a destructive force. There is a lot at stake.

As the son of a European father and American mother who both lived through World War ll, I learned that there is no heroism in war, only destruction and the loss of valuable life. Another global war will likely do more damage than the over 60 million people killed during the Second World War.

After the war ended, Jung remained cautious about the future. In an interview with Dr. Richard Evans of the University of Houston in 1957, he said:

The world hangs by a thin thread, and that thread is the psyche of man. Nowadays, we are not threatened by elemental catastrophes; there is no such thing in nature as an H-Bomb. That is all man's doing. WE are the great danger. The psyche is the great danger. What if something goes wrong with the psyche?

Everywhere people are active and engaged, so are their personalities. That is why there are so many useful applications of Jung's model. You can use it to understand the polarities in politics, organizational culture, science, sports, education, economics, leadership, music, art, medicine, counseling, management, religion, teamwork, and parenting, amongst others. The list is endless. And these principles are just as applicable to teams and organizations as they are to individuals.

One does wonder though, why do polarities exist in the first place? That is the subject we turn to in the next chapter.

Chapter 2

The Purpose of Polarities

It was the best of times, it was the worst of times,
It was the age of wisdom, it was the age of foolishness,
It was the epoch of belief, it was the epoch of incredulity,
It was the season of Light, it was the season of Darkness,
It was the spring of hope, it was the winter of despair,
We had everything before us, we had nothing before us,
We were all going direct to Heaven, we were all going direct the other way.

~ Charles Dickens, Tale of Two Cities, 1859

With these pairs of opposites, Charles Dickens describes the situation in London and Paris during the French Revolution in 1789. His novel tells the story of a time when society was polarized. A period of conflict and chaos where despair and happiness existed side by side.

You may ask, how can this be true? It does not make sense. How could such opposites exist together? How could anyone live in such a world? The truth is, we live in such a world all the time. That is why the words of Charles Dickens continue to be valid today. It is part of the human experience.

Through the ages, many philosophers from many continents have embraced the notion that we live in a world of contradictions where truth is found in paradox, in opposing statements that are equally true. Consider the statement "We are all created equal." It is certainly true that we should all have equal and inalienable human rights. But the opposite, "We are all created unequal," is also true. No person is the same; every one of us is unique and has unique gifts and talents.

Or consider the current scientific method where the following paradigm tends to prevail: *"If you can't measure it, it doesn't exist."* This implies that if you cannot measure something, it is nothing but an artfully crafted delusion. But the opposite is also true. I have never heard of a measure for love and yet most people would agree love exists and has real significance. It is also entirely possible that something is not measurable with the technology we have now, but it will be in the future. People thought the earth was flat until the telescope proved otherwise. When dealing with polarities and paradox, I have found the following principle to be most relevant:

The role of human consciousness is to discern WHEN, WHERE and HOW one statement or idea is true, AND WHEN, WHERE and HOW the opposing statement or idea is also true—not WHETHER either one is true to the exclusion of the other.

The polarity of night and day is an excellent example of how this principle works in practice.

What if Night and Day Excluded Each Other?

If we lived on a planet where it was only day, life would not be possible as we know it. The sun would scorch most plants, shrubs, and trees. The earth would be barren. On the other hand, if it were only night, photosynthesis could not occur, and life would also be impossible. Natural resources that result from billions of years of photosynthesis such as oil, gold, diamonds, or coal simply would not exist.

We can learn several other important things about polarities from this example of night and day. For instance, when it is day on one half of the planet, it is night on the opposite half. Periods of light follow periods of darkness. And they never conflict with each other so that one thing you can be certain of every day is that the sun will rise in the morning and set in the evening. There also is no right or wrong in either night or day. The harmonic rhythm of night and day is the powerful harmonic balance that produces abundant life on our planet.

We can also learn a few things from this example on how polarities are NOT supposed to interact. For instance, what if either night or day tried to prevail over the other? Or worse, what if we had one group of people on Earth that only believed night to be true, and another group that only believed day to be true. Would either of them be right? This touches on the problem of absolutes. As soon as we start believing in the absoluteness of one pole in a polarity, we fall into a trap. When we exclude the other, we polarize. We get trapped in "either-or" instead of "both-and" reasoning. It is a dangerous illusion and much more widespread than you would think.

In the Star Wars Movie *Revenge of the Sith* there is a scene where Anakin (who later becomes Darth Vader) says to Obi-Wan Kenobi, *"If you are not with me, you are my enemy."* To which Obi-Wan Kenobi responds, *"Only a Sith deals in absolutes."* What does this mean? The Sith were the Order of the Dark Side that fought the Jedi Order, and it was in this scene that Obi-Wan Kenobi discovered that Anakin had become a Dark Lord. Dealing in absolutes is very tempting and sometimes even necessary. In practical everyday life, we must make choices. There are, for instance, laws that determine whether something is legal or illegal. In the United States, it is an absolute that it is unlawful to drive on the left side of the road. However, when we find ourselves thinking of someone else as either right or wrong, good or bad and want to attack them for their truth, we fall into a trap that leads to a Sith way of thinking, with destructive and potentially evil results. It is for this reason that the constitution protects freedom of speech.

An example of "both-and" reasoning that produces positive results is found in an old Disney movie where the wizard Merlin teaches a young Arthur about the laws of polarities:

Left and right
Like day and night
That's what makes the world go round

In and out
Thin and stout
That's what makes the world go round
For every up, there is a down
For every square, there is a round
For every high, there is a low
For every to there is a fro
To and fro
Stop and go
That's what makes the world go round
(Song by the Sherman Brothers, The Sword in the Stone, 1963)

These examples demonstrate that the following principles are at work when it comes to polarities:
1. Polarities are pairs of opposites that are interdependent.
2. Polarities are intended to harmonize and give each other space and time to "do their job."
3. It is not a question of whether one or the other is true, but of when, where and how each of them is true.
4. There is no right or wrong, good or bad in either pole of a polarity. There is only balance or imbalance.
5. The power of polarities is to energize and transform life, to "make the world go around."

Try a similar exercise with other polarities and see if these principles still apply, for instance:
- Light and Dark
- Hot and Cold
- Same and Different
- High and Low

Polarities are Related to Their Opposite

An interesting and undeniable quality of polarities—and this needs some clarification—is that they are not only opposite but that they are related and interdependent. This means that one cannot exist without the other and it explains why polarizing by thinking in absolutes is unproductive because you are separating two things that below together.

Night, for example, is understood and defined just as much by what it is as by what it is not. Night is defined by the absence of day; day by the absence of night. And this means that one cannot exist without the other.

The song *Let Her Go* by Passenger poignantly captures the human experience of this in these lyrics:

> You only need the light when it's burning low,
> Only miss the sun when it starts to snow,
> Only know you've been high when you're feeling low,
> Only hate the road when you're missing home,
> Only know you love her when you let her go,
> And you let her go...

Why Do Polarities Exist?

What sets humans apart from animals is that humans have *Ego Consciousness*. What does this mean? Consciousness is a complicated subject. To explain why polarities exist and what that has to do with human consciousness I will try to simplify.

A relatively simple but useful model of consciousness identifies three levels or stages:
1. Single Consciousness
2. Dual Consciousness
3. Transcendent Consciousness

In the 9th century, Zen master Qingyuan Weixin explained these stages as follows:

Before you study Zen, mountains are mountains and rivers are rivers; while you are studying Zen, mountains are no longer mountains and rivers are no longer rivers; but once you have had enlightenment, mountains are once again mountains and rivers again rivers.
(Suzuki, 1926, p. 24)

The ancient Greek philosopher Heraclitus also liked to use the example of a river. In single consciousness, all we see is the river. In dual consciousness, we no longer see the river as a river but as flowing water. We realize the river never remains the same from one moment to the next. We arrive at a place where we see it either as a river or not as a river; by definition, it has to be one of the two. This is what is called "either-or" thinking, where something has to be either this or that, but cannot be both. In transcendent consciousness, we see the river again but also know it consists of flowing water. It is both river and not-river. This is called "both-and" thinking, and as a result, our consciousness is expanded and enriched.

The American poet T.S. Eliot summarizes this aptly when he writes in the poem *Little Gidding*:

And the end of all our exploring will be to arrive where we started and know the place for the first time.

Knowing the place and expressing it in art is what great artists like the Dutch painter Vincent van Gogh have achieved. A good illustration of this is Van Gogh's famous 1889 painting *The Starry Night*. He did not set out to paint a realistic image of a starry night; he wanted to portray it as he saw it in his mind's eye.

Throughout history, many schools of thought have examined the dynamic transition between these three stages of consciousness. The ancient Greek philosopher Heraclitus and the German philosopher Hegel amongst others identify three stages of development that together form a "dialectic" or dynamic interaction between the poles of polarities. A dialectic is a process through which opposites come together, and resolve their differences.

In the first stage of the dialectic process, something comes into being which is called the "thesis." In the second stage, it is reacted to, contradicted and negated by its "antithesis." In the third stage, the tension between the two is reconciled and transcended by the "synthesis" of the two.

The stages of the dialectic correspond with the three levels of consciousness.

1. Single Consciousness	1. Thesis
2. Dual Consciousness	2. Thesis vs. Antithesis
3. Transcendent Consciousness	3. Synthesis

An example that is often used to illustrate the dialectic is the birth and raising of a child. In its first years, the child and the parents are "one," and the child is more or less obedient. That is the thesis or single consciousness. In puberty, a child tends to rebel against the parents to form his or her own identity and authority. That is the antithesis or dual consciousness. And as an adult, the child will hopefully have his or her own identity that transcends the parents but will no longer live in rebellion but rather in reconciliation with his or her parents. That is the synthesis or transcendent stage of consciousness.

A second example is the verb "to be." Its antithesis is "not to be." The synthesis is "to become."

What is important to realize about the third stage of consciousness is that it will both *transcend* and *include* the previous stages. The child in adulthood has his or her own identity but is still the child of the parents.

A third example comes from my economics studies. The word economy is a combination of the Greek words *oikos* (house) and *nemein* (to manage), i.e., the management of a household. Economics is the science that studies the production, distribution, and consumption of goods and services. In the most primitive economies, a family would hunt or grow its own food and manage its household on its own. But as villages developed, families traded food. A single family no longer had to produce everything it needed. However, trading food became difficult as families started producing different kinds of goods. If one family produced milk, the other meat, and yet another potatoes, the trading of goods became increasingly more complicated. The synthesis was found in the invention of a unitary mode of exchange: coinage.

A fourth example is the growth of a tree. First, there is the seed (thesis). When planted, the seed grows into a tree (antithesis). But not until the tree develops its own fruit does it achieve a synthesis with its original seed.

Transcendence is the Key to Transformation

One becomes two, two becomes three, and out of the third comes the one as the fourth.
(Axiom of Maria)

When the tension between the opposite poles of a polarity becomes too high to sustain, there is a need for transcendence, for reconciling and uniting the opposites. The process of transcendence results in transformation.

This is a four-step cyclical process that Jung referred to as the Axiom of Maria: out of the first comes the opposite as the second, and out of the first and second comes the third which resolves the conflict. And out of the third comes the fourth which is the next "first," the new life, the transformation, after which the completed cycle recommences.

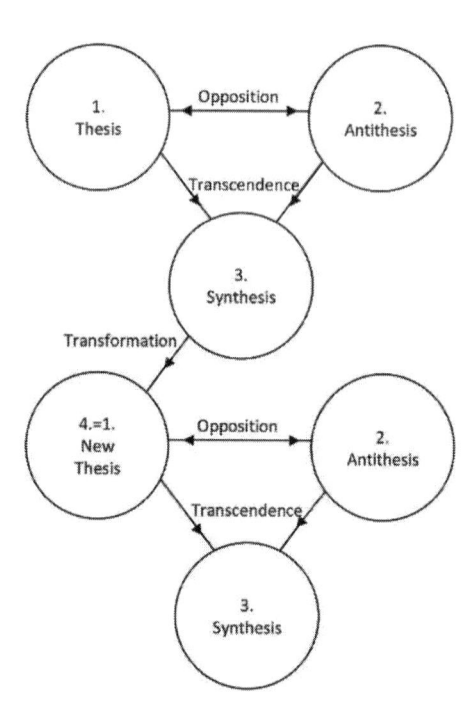

But how does transcendent consciousness bring transformation about? Transformation is the creation of something new out of something that exists, out of an existing polarity. For example, an electron and a proton are transformed into an atom through the "reconciling" or "unifying" force that we call electromagnetism. Likewise, a human egg and sperm cell transform into a child through the "reconciling" or "unifying" process we call reproduction, where human magnetism is the unifying force.

If we take a look at the example of the atom, we now know through the theory of quantum mechanics how electromagnetism functions as the transcendent function in the formation of an atom out of protons and electrons (and neutrons, but as the name suggests, they are neutral).

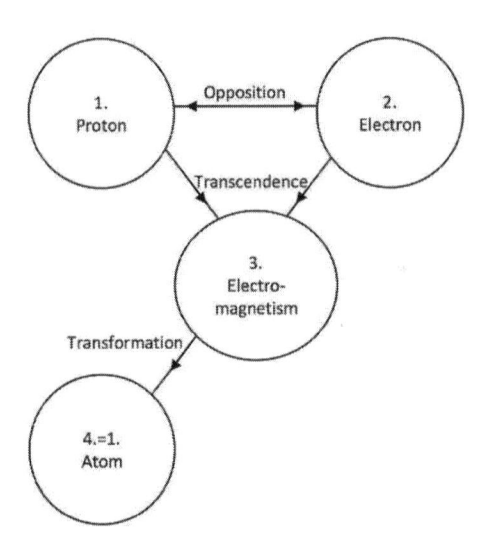

```
        1. Proton  ←— Opposition —→  2. Electron
                    ↘ Transcendence ↙
                      3. Electro-magnetism
                    ↙ Transformation
                4.=1. Atom
```

This is a cyclical process as well. At one point the "new" meets its opposite, and out of this opposition, something new is created. In the case of atoms, they merge to create molecules. In our own human procreation, sperm cells meet egg cells and children are conceived. The children become adults with their own reproductive organs and the cycle repeats.

What happens next is that this cyclical process propagates other cyclical processes. Individual humans together form the human species just as individual molecules form matter. And that serves the next purpose and the next.

This means all of nature is involved in the cyclical process of transformation. But, as stated earlier, humans fulfill a special role because we possess ego consciousness, which we can use to either create or destroy. Consciousness gives us the ability to reflect on this process and influence it.

It is the purpose of polarities to transcend and transform. It is their destination to make this happen. It is in fact what leads to happiness. Robert Johnson, a Jungian analyst, and author, once told me that this is the origin of the word "happiness." Happiness occurs when life's opposites meet in oneself and make life "happen" in a meaningful way. There is no simpler—and no more difficult and painful way—to be happy. Simple because it is a four-step process. Difficult and painful because one must endure the tension between opposites.

This process is inevitable; it is the nature of our existence and of our consciousness. We cannot help but progress through these stages and experience cycles of rebirth and transformation. It instills in us the right kind of humility because the transformation occurs from the unconscious over which we have no conscious control. All we can do is facilitate this process within ourselves. Our greatest pitfall in this task is to get stuck in dual consciousness, in "either-or" thinking.

The great challenge is that the instinctual nature of polarities is to exist in dual consciousness, because the poles are per definition opposite. Or as Jung wrote in *Psychological Types*:

> *Each standpoint denies the principal value of the other. The more resolutely the adherents of either standpoint identify themselves with it,*

the more they strive, with the best intentions perhaps, to force it on another, the more they violate the other's supreme value.
(Jung, CW 6, § 32)

Restricted by its own limited worldview, each pole of a polarity cannot see how it can co-exist with the other. In our world, as we know it, this attitude has resulted in conflicts, wars, even genocide. It is not difficult to see where this ends. Or as Mahatma Gandhi purportedly once said: *"An eye for an eye and a tooth for a tooth will make the whole world blind and toothless."* One would think that there has to be a better and more conscious way to deal with polarities in life.

The Role of the Unconscious in the Union of Opposites

The main question then is how to progress from dual to transcendent consciousness? Or rather: how to allow the process of transcendence to happen? Because it really is something beyond our conscious control, it is something that happens by holding the tension between the opposites, by being in balance as well as we can. This is exactly what Merlin teaches the young Arthur in the 1963 Disney movie when he says:

Left and right
Like day and night
That's what makes the world go round

The psychological term Jung coined for this is *"coniunctio oppositorum,"* Latin for "the joining together of opposites." It is the reconciliation and unification of polarities with the corresponding birth of new life and a new consciousness. This development of new consciousness is something Jung described as follows:

> *Suddenly there is a flash of association between two apparently disconnected and widely separated ideas, and this has the effect of releasing a latent tension. Such a moment often works like a revelation. In every case, it seems to be the discharge of energy-tension, whether external or internal, which produces consciousness.*
> (Jung, CW 17, § 207)

What is interesting about Jung's discovery is that this consciousness arises from the unconscious. It is unconscious content that is made conscious through the dialectical process described earlier in this chapter:

> *For indeed our consciousness does not create itself— it wells up from unknown depths. In childhood it awakens gradually, and all through life it wakes each morning out of the depths of sleep from an unconscious condition. It is like a child that is born daily out of the primordial womb of the unconscious. In fact, closer investigation reveals that it is not only influenced by the unconscious but continually emerges out of it in the form of numberless spontaneous ideas and sudden flashes of thought.*
> (Jung, CW 11, § 935)

In other words, as human beings, we are vehicles of consciousness. When we are able to hold and sustain the tension within a polarity in our consciousness, the unconscious will present a new insight, a transcendent and unifying process to our consciousness. Such epiphanies raise our level consciousness from dual to transcendent.

Transcendent Consciousness in Abraham Lincoln's Gettysburg Address

Former U.S. president Abraham Lincoln understood the power of polarities. His Gettysburg Address is a great example of transcendent consciousness. His speech was part of the ceremony which dedicated the cemetery to the many thousands of soldiers who had died in the Battle of Gettysburg during the Civil War (1861-1865). This battle is regarded as the turning point of this war.

I believe that not only was the battle itself a turning point but so was Lincoln's speech. It reminded the North, and its soldiers of the purpose of this terrible war fought between brothers and families within one nation.

It was the middle of the Civil War, and Lincoln used this moment to explain what he thought was at stake. He was not the main speaker at the event, but was asked to "set apart these grounds to their sacred use by a few appropriate remarks." His short 2-minute delivery was so powerful that it has gone down in history as one of the greatest speeches ever given by a U.S. president.

His speech starts with a thesis, followed by an antithesis, which he then connects to form a synthesis out of which comes the next thesis in what is a classic four-step dialectic cycle. The speech was written with transcendent consciousness and directed the listener towards the new reality that it could create. Allow me to take you through the entire speech step-by-step.

First, Lincoln posits the thesis. For this he refers to the Declaration of Independence 87 years earlier (in 1776):

Four score and seven years ago our fathers brought forth, on this continent, a new nation, conceived in Liberty, and dedicated to the proposition that all men are created equal.

Next, the antithesis follows with an account of the terrible conflict of the Civil War:

Now we are engaged in a great civil war, testing whether that nation, or any nation so conceived and so dedicated, can long endure. We are met on a great battlefield of that war. We have come to dedicate a portion of that field, as a final resting place for those who here gave their lives that that nation might live. It is altogether fitting and proper that we should do this.

Then he does something remarkable, something that must have come to him in a flash of insight. Instead of dedicating the cemetery, he appeals to the audience to dedicate themselves to the cemetery, more specifically to the cause for which these soldiers had died. Note how Lincoln uses the words "rather" and "but" to denote transcendence:

> *But, in a larger sense, we cannot dedicate—we cannot consecrate—we cannot hallow—this ground. The brave men, living and dead, who struggled here, have consecrated it, far above our poor power to add or detract. The world will little note, nor long remember what we say here, but it can never forget what they did here. It is for us the living, rather, to be dedicated here to the unfinished work which they who fought here have thus far so nobly advanced. It is rather for us to be here dedicated to the great task remaining before us—that from these honored dead we take increased devotion to that cause for which they gave the last full measure of devotion—that we here highly resolve that these dead shall not have died in vain.*

And he ends with the fourth step, a vision of transformation, of a new birth that this conflict must inevitably lead to as a result of the transcendence in the previous paragraph:

> *That this nation, under God, shall have a new birth of freedom—and that government of the people, by the people, for the people, shall not perish from the earth.*

The Battle of Gettysburg ended on the Fourth of July, the date the Declaration of Independence was signed in 1776. This must have inspired Lincoln in writing this speech. He delivered it on November 19, 1863, and the next day all the newspapers printed it. It must have been an inspirational motivation for the Union Army: from that moment on they knew what they were fighting for. A year and a half later the 11 Confederate states and 23 Union states concluded a war that is estimated to have resulted in between 620,000 and 750,000 casualties, more American casualties than in both World Wars combined. The military strength of the Confederate states, led by General Robert E. Lee, was so overwhelming that the northern Union states lost most of the battles in the first two years of the war. It is said that the turning point for the Union was the Battle of Gettysburg, but from a psychological perspective, I believe it was Abraham Lincoln's speech that made the difference.

Chapter 3

Towards a More Conscious Ego

> *Anyone who has any ego-consciousness at all takes it for granted that he knows himself. But the ego knows only its own contents, not the unconscious and its contents.*
>
> ~ C.G. Jung, CW 10, § 491

The ego is a limited but essential center of consciousness. Its role in creating higher levels of consciousness is crucial because it is only through the ego that the connection between the conscious and unconscious parts of the psyche can be made. A well-developed, conscious ego has the strength to sustain the tension of polarities, between consciousness and the unconscious.

Jung stressed the importance of the ego as follows:

> *The important fact about consciousness is that nothing can be conscious without an ego to which it refers. If something is not related to the ego then it is not conscious. Therefore, you can define consciousness as a relation of psychic facts to the ego.*

(Jung, CW 18, § 18)

An analogy is often made between the ego and a sailing boat. A boat that cannot cope with winds and other forces of nature is "weak," which is analogous to an ego that cannot cope with the "forces of the unconscious" and is therefore considered undeveloped. The boat will be thrown around by the elements. In contrast, a boat that can handle the winds and the elements and bring the boat into the safe harbor is analogous to a developed and strong ego that can handle the "forces of the unconscious." This analogy was probably born in Jungian circles because Jung himself liked to go sailing from his family home on Lake Zürich in Switzerland.

How can one develop a conscious, healthy and strong ego? One of the most useful models to help understand how polarities interact, is the infinity symbol, also called the Lemniscate, first discovered by the Swiss mathematician, Jakob Bernoulli in 1694. It was introduced to me by one of my teachers, Robert Stamboliev (1992), to describe the ebb-and-flow between sub-personalities. It is, however, an old geometric model used in many schools of thought. I have adapted it here for the purpose of understanding how the polarities in the psyche interact to develop ego consciousness.

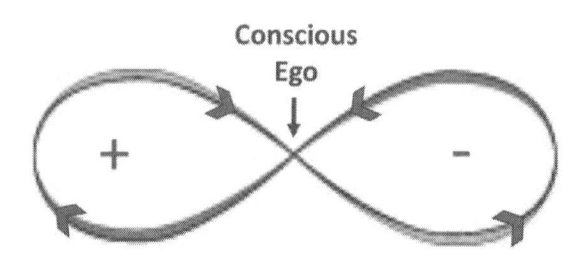

The infinity symbol represents the eternal rhythmic flow within a pair of polarities. Think of strong-vulnerable, dream-reality, sadness-joy, courage-fear, power-love, practical-visionary, conservative-progressive, warm-cold… The list is endless.

This vacillating between the opposites and being tossed back and forth means being contained in the opposites. They become a vessel in which what was previously one thing, and now another is vibrating so that the painful suspension between opposites gradually changes into the bilateral activity of the point in the center.
(Jung, CW 14, § 296)

The point in the center that Jung refers to is the conscious ego. The conscious ego observes and facilitates this process, without choosing sides and without allowing one of the poles in the polarity to dominate it. It delves into one side after the other.

This center of consciousness can be developed in individuals (the ego), teams and organizations. The effects are powerful. Sports teams, for example, can become like the sailing boat that can handle a storm. The stress of an important game need not impede performance (which it usually does). Instead it can become a vehicle for high performance. Once one knows how to handle the strong winds of a storm, it only serves to make the "boat" slice through the waves and achieve its destination faster.

A wonderful example of how to harness the power of polarities, is the creative process followed by Walt Disney when he worked on a new movie project. Disney believed: *"If you can dream it, you can do it!"* He would not stop at dreaming. He used three processes (dreaming, planning, and criticism) within an interactive triangle to realize his dreams:

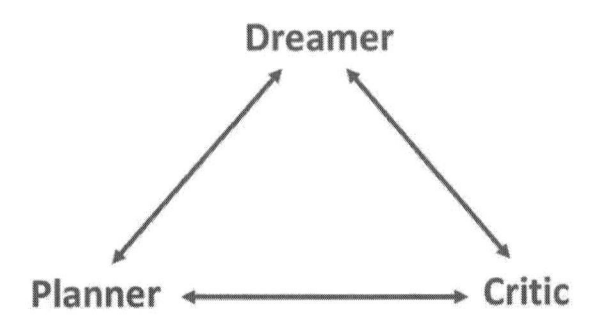

Dreamer

Planner ⟷ **Critic**

Disney had the insight to give each of these processes its own space and time. The dreamer in him would visualize a new movie in great detail. The planner in him would then figure out how to make it happen. The critic would then examine the plan to find the flaws. The planner would either resolve the flaws or take the issue back to the dreamer to modify the original vision. After this process, Disney would step back, consider what these different voices in him had said, and make decisions from there.

There are some interesting conclusions we can draw from the Lemniscate process regarding the harmonization of polarities in individuals, teams, organizations, or even in societies globally.

For polarities to balance and connect harmoniously, they need to:
1. Alternate in a rhythmic way, like a pendulum, without going outside the circumference of the circle, i.e., without going to extremes and splitting off.
2. Be met and dealt with sequentially in time and space, without missing either (like traveling around the circumference of a circle).
3. Have a center (or conscious ego) in which they can connect, in which the movement goes from one polarity to the other.

If we can do this consciously within ourselves, or in the team of which we are a part, the impact will be transformative. In the case of Walt Disney, the polarities of the Dreamer, Planner, and Critic were transformed into the creation of a new movie in which they were all transcended and included.

A conscious ego will be involved in doing the following:
1. Taking time to explore a situation from all points of views.
2. Avoiding going to extremes and choosing to stay within certain boundaries.

3. Becoming clear about its purpose (represented by the center of the circle) and making choices that are connected to this center.

Finding the Center

If you try to draw an Infinity Symbol and then another and another directly on top of each other, you might find that it is hard to do accurately.

Now try it again, but first, draw a circle with a dot in the middle and then draw three or more Infinity Symbols inside the circle. You will probably discover that the circle and the dot simplify this exercise and that the results are more symmetrical and accurate.

The same principle applies to our individual psyche: connecting polarities is easier once you have a center. The center is the place where the conscious ego finds purpose and belonging. Without a center, without a clear purpose, the ego goes adrift and cannot develop a healthy, conscious relationship with the polarities it is working with. Finding your center is essential for psychological growth.

Walt Disney found his center: his purpose was simply to "Make People Happy." It was his guiding principle, his point of reference, the heart of the circle in which he operated. Whenever he had to choose between the dreamer, the planner, and the critic, he asked himself, "How can I best make people happy?"
Unlike the Disney Company of today, his aim was not to "maximize shareholder value." That wasn't his reason for making movies and is not a valid purpose in this context. A legitimate purpose is one that is of service to others and creates value for potential customers. This is why Jack Welch, the former CEO of General Electric, said in an interview for a *Financial Times* series on the "Future of Capitalism" (2009):

On the face of it, shareholder value is the dumbest idea in the world. Shareholder value is a result, not a strategy... Your main constituencies are your employees, your customers, and your products.

Finding your center is about knowing yourself. "The essence of knowledge is self-knowledge," said Plato. *"Know Thyself"* was inscribed in the temple of Apollo at Delphi. Have you ever wondered why ancient Greek philosophers like Plato and Heraclitus adopted the adage *"Know Thyself"* as the foundation of all knowledge? They believed that by knowing oneself one would know the world, and this has been an important principle in Western philosophy ever since. Carl Jung is no exception. His life's work was centered on helping us know ourselves, and with this, he meant: finding your place and purpose in the world.

The consequences of not finding a center or the wrong center are damaging. Therefore, we need a conscious ego. Without a conscious ego, the polarities in the psyche cannot harmonize; instead, they polarize. The price of such a polarization is significant, or as Jung said:

Today humanity, as never before, is split into two apparently irreconcilable halves. The psychological rule says that when an inner situation is not made conscious, it happens outside, as fate. That is to say, when the individual remains undivided and does not become conscious of his inner contradictions, the world must perforce act out the conflict and be torn into opposing halves.
(Jung, CW 9ii, § 128)

This means that in order for conflict to be creative and not destructive an effort needs to be made to avoid reverting from dual to single consciousness, but instead to sustain the tension until transcendent consciousness arises. This becomes much easier if there is a center, if one has a sense of why one exists, and a sense of purpose.

Polarities in Life

For further clarification, let us examine some important polarities that we encounter in society. What are some of the great paradoxes? What is their nature and how can we deal with them more effectively and with more consciousness? The examples below demonstrate that solving the paradox in one polarity automatically leads to the next.

Freedom vs. Limitation
Freedom without limitation leads to chaos, limitation without freedom to slavery. One cannot exist without the other. There is an inherent contradiction in the notion of freedom. If everyone is free, what happens when we interfere with the freedom of others? This paradox can be resolved by choosing to accept limitation through an act of free will. But how can a society do this?

In order to do this as a society, we need to deal with the next polarity:

Individual vs. Collective
We were all born as individuals. There is and will only ever be one "you." On the other hand, the individual who lives without the collective can be selfish, egotistic, and lonely. The contradiction inherent in the individual is that he or she needs others to be him or herself. For example, we were born as individuals, but we were also born into families, and without these families, we would not have survived. This paradox can be resolved only by choosing to submit as individuals to certain collective choices. This is the paradox the ancient Greeks tried to solve by inventing democracy, and which we are still trying to solve in the modern democracies of today.

To do this, we need to deal with the next polarity:

Equality vs. Diversity

Let us assume that we were all born equal. The United States Declaration of Independence says, "We hold these truths to be self-evident, that all men are created equal." So how can we provide for the individual in a collective? By allowing for diversity. Diversity in talent, ethnicity, drive, passion, Intelligence Quotient (IQ), Emotional Quotient (EQ). In such a society, a social fabric is needed with ethical and moral values that allow differences to co-exist, as well as laws that protect those values. How can we disagree fundamentally, and still co-exist together? Charles Darwin and other scientists who have studied the evolution of our planet realized that diversity is the key to sustainability and the survival of a species because it enables it to adapt and change. Without it, the species becomes extinct.

You have probably experienced these paradoxes in your own life. Whether it is Freedom vs. Limitation, Individual vs. Collective, or Equality vs. Diversity. Jung's psychology can be helpful to unravel the conundrums raised by these and other paradoxes, because like no other psychologist before or after him, he acted in accordance with the hypothesis that polarities exist in the human psyche and that the process of denying and misunderstanding them is the source of human suffering. He described neurosis as an imbalance in a psychological polarity and the remedy as a balance, centering and grounding the polarities.

In my work with individuals and teams I have seen that if we can connect these polarities to their higher purpose, these troubles can be overcome. Contrary to what Hollywood tells us, romance is not about making the other person happy, or having "your needs met." It is about two people respecting and serving the higher purpose of their bond. It is about two people transcending their differences and creating something that is more meaningful than their individual lives, and individual needs could ever be. A relationship thus becomes a commitment to the development of consciousness.

Even though this is just a prelude, I hope that I have illustrated how, time and time again, polarities are intended to move us from single consciousness to dual consciousness and then to transcendent consciousness. The fundamental polarities of consciousness and their power can be found in the personality, and that is where Carl Jung's work on personality types is so valuable. But before we delve into what the polarities in the personality are, it is useful to look at who Jung was and what internal and external events led to his remarkable discoveries.

CHAPTER 4

SHOULDERS TO STAND ON

If I have seen further, it is by standing on the shoulders of giants.
~ Isaac Newton, 1675

Every human achievement is the result of a human achievement that preceded it. Since as humans we are endowed with a limited perspective or worldview, it is only by standing on the shoulders of giants and applying the experience and knowledge of those who went before us that we can "see further" too. Then, by integrating the work of previous generations in the here and now, something of quality and sustainability is created for future generations.

Just as we can now stand on the shoulders of Carl Jung and others who preceded us, Jung himself stood on the shoulders of Freud and many others who preceded him and influenced his thoughts, like the great German philosophers Arthur Schopenhauer and

Immanuel Kant. So, to better understand his work, we need to understand how it evolved from his life story.

Carl Jung

Carl Jung was born in 1875 in Switzerland as the son of Paul Jung and Emilie Preiswerk. His mother came from a family of Protestant pastors. His father was a pastor in the Swiss Reformed Church, which had been founded by Zwingli, a leader of the Reformation in Switzerland. Religion inevitably played a significant role in Jung's upbringing and the formation of his character. He struggled, however, with his father's rigid and dogmatic approach to faith because he did not feel it was alive. He wanted a living faith, and this sparked his interest in the role of religion in the psychology of people. However, Jung's father unquestioningly adhered to the very letter of the teachings of his church.

In his autobiography originally published in 1961, *Memories, Dreams, Reflections* (1989), Jung writes about the difficulty of talking to his father about religion:

> *I would have liked to lay my religious difficulties before him and ask him for advice, but I did not do so because it seemed to me that I knew in advance what he would be obliged to reply out of respect for his office.*
> (Chapter II: The School Years)

And he saw how his father suffered from upholding his faith:

> *My memory of my father is of a sufferer... The words of Galatians 2:20: "I live, yet not I, but Christ liveth in me," never penetrated his mind in their full significance, for any thinking about religious matters sent shudders of horror through him. He wanted to rest content with faith... Blind acceptance never leads to a solution; at best it leads only to a standstill and is paid for heavily in the next generation.*
> (Chapter VII: The Work)

After having a religious experience of his own, Jung concluded about his father:

> ... he had never experienced the miracle of grace which heals all and makes all comprehensible. He had taken the Bible's commandments as his guide; he believed in God as the Bible prescribed and as his forefathers had taught him. But he did not know the immediate living God who stands, omnipotent and free, above His Bible and His Church, who calls upon man to partake of His freedom... In His trial of human courage God refuses to abide by traditions, no matter how sacred.
> (Chapter II: The School Years)

His mother was quite the opposite of his father. Whereas his father was staunch in his beliefs and more of an introverted scholar, his mother was extraverted and jovial:

> My mother was a very good mother to me. She had a hearty animal warmth, cooked wonderfully, and was most companionable and pleasant. She was very stout, and a ready listener. She also liked to talk, and her chatter was like the gay splashing of a fountain.
> (Chapter II: The School Years)

Jung also seemed to have inherited his uncanny intuition from his mother:

> In the course of my life it has often happened to me that I suddenly knew something which I really could not know at all. The knowledge came to me as though it were my own idea. It was the same with my mother. She did not know what she was saying; it was like a voice wielding absolute authority, which said exactly what fitted the situation.
> (Chapter II: The School Years)

As a teenager, Jung went to the Gymnasium in Basel, a high school that prepared students for university and included the study of Latin and Ancient Greek. After graduating, he enrolled at the University of Basel as a medical student. At the time psychiatry as a medical discipline was looked down upon by the medical profession, and yet Jung chose to pursue a career in it. He had a great interest in both biology and philosophy, and for him, psychiatry was the discipline in which both came together. Jung wrote:

> *My heart suddenly began to pound. I had to stand up and draw a deep breath. My excitement was intense, for it had become clear to me, in a flash of illumination that for me the only possible goal was psychiatry.*
> (Chapter III: The Student Years)

In 1900, at 25 years of age, he began working at the Burghölzli psychiatric hospital in Zürich as a research scientist under the supervision of Dr. Eugen Bleuler (1857-1939), an eminent psychiatrist who acted as a mentor for a still young Jung. His career developed quickly. In 1902, he was awarded a Ph.D. from the University of Zürich, and in 1905 he became a lecturer there as well as a senior physician at the Burghölzli clinic. In 1909, at the age of 34, he left the clinic to start his own practice and conduct research.

In 1903, he married Emma Rauschenbach, the daughter of a wealthy Swiss industrialist, and they had five children: four daughters, and one son. They remained married for 52 years until Emma passed away in 1955. Jung died six years later in 1961 at the age of 86.

Why Jung Wrote *Psychological Types*

Like many great thinkers, Jung tried to solve a puzzle, a need he perceived in society. The problem he most wanted to understand and address with his book *Psychological Types* (1921) was the suffering caused by political, religious and philosophical misunderstandings, strife and conflict, and ensuing wars. This is not surprising given the time in which he lived and the two World Wars he witnessed.

The inner and outer events that led Jung to formulate a theory of personality types can be summarized by what Jung writes in the introduction to *Psychological Types*:

> *In my practical medical work, I have long been struck by the fact that besides the many individual differences in human psychology there are also typical differences. These insights will, I hope, help to clarify the dilemma which… especially in the personal relations of human beings with one another, has led and still continues to lead to misunderstanding and discord.*
> (Jung, CW 6, § 1)

In the years preceding the publication of *Psychological Types*, Jung encountered a significant amount of "misunderstanding and discord" himself. In 1914, he ended a long and fruitful collaboration with Sigmund Freud. That same year he witnessed the eruption of the the First World War and the horrible devastation it brought to the European continent. These two events initiated a seven-year period of deep introspection and "inner work" which resulted in his work on typology, *Psychological Types*.

Jung was a man who had frequent visions. One such vision was a premonition or "waking dream" relating to World War I:

> *While I was alone on a journey, I was suddenly seized by an overpowering vision: I saw a monstrous flood covering all the northern and low-lying lands between the North Sea and the Alps. When it came up to Switzerland I saw that the mountains grew higher and higher to protect our country. I realized that a frightful catastrophe was in progress. I saw the mighty yellow waves, the floating rubble of civilization, and the drowned bodies of uncounted thousands. Then the whole sea turned to blood.*
> (Jung, 1989, Chapter VI: Confrontation with the Unconscious)

This vision deeply troubled him because he could not understand its significance at the time. It was not until the outbreak of nationalism and extremism in Germany that led to WWI that he understood what it meant. It was a symbolical narrative of the horrific conflict that was to unfold. Fortunately, his personality was endowed with enough intuition to understand its meaning.

These conflicts and wars, as well as his personal conflict with Freud and the end of their relationship, motivated Jung to gain an understanding of the typological differences between people.

Carl Jung And Sigmund Freud

Jung met Freud on February 27, 1907, in Vienna. Jung was 31 and Freud 50. At their first meeting, they talked for thirteen hours straight. For Jung, Freud was someone who *"was way ahead of me."* He felt he could learn a lot from him and decided to *"stick around."* They corresponded and collaborated extensively, and Freud viewed Jung as his most talented, inventive, and original student.

Many of Freud's ideas were validated by research performed by Jung using word association tests. Soon Jung became his protégé, and Freud saw him as the leader of his movement and heir to his psychoanalytical work. This was formalized in Jung's appointment as the first president (and Chairman for Life) of the International Psychoanalytical Association (IPA) in 1910. Freud founded the IPA to advance his psychoanalytical method through an international organization. It still exists today and currently has 12,000 members from all over the world.

Their friendship and collaboration did not last much beyond that point, as considerable differences arose between them. Freud considered repressed and unconsciously expressed sexuality to be the driving forces behind human behavior. In line with this, he coined the term "Oedipus Complex," after the Greek myth of the youth Oedipus who unknowingly kills his father and marries his mother. For Freud, the unconscious functioned as a repository of repressed experiences only, especially around sexuality.

Carl Jung developed a decidedly different perspective. Jung developed a different point of view. He could not accept Freud's insistence that the Oedipus Complex was the singular theory of psychoanalysis. That Freud had this point of view was not so surprising view given the sexual repression that characterized the 19th-century Victorian era in which they lived. For him, sexuality was only one of many forces driving human behavior. He saw the unconscious as not only a place for repressed experiences and mental illness but as the ultimate source of all psychological life, healing, and personal growth.

It was an ideological struggle, unfortunately, one of many throughout history. And as always it was based on fundamentally different and mutually exclusive worldviews, rooted in their individual personalities. Since neither he nor Freud was fully aware of their typological differences, they became irreconcilable, causing the breakdown in their communication and collaboration.

Jung resigned as president of the IPA in 1914, just before World War I erupted. This devastating break-up disillusioned both men. Yet, at the end of their lives, they were both able to express a deep respect for each other. Jung wrote in a letter in 1957: *"I cannot, despite my resentment towards him, fail to recognize his importance... without Freud the key (to my work) would have been entirely missing for me."*

Group photo in front of Clark University (1909).
Front row: Sigmund Freud, G. Stanley Hall, C. G. Jung.
Back row: Abraham A. Brill, Ernest Jones, Sándor Ferenczi.

Confrontation with the Unconscious

The break-up between Jung and Freud began a period of seclusion for Jung in which he was thrown back on himself and was forced to face his own unconscious and work on his own healing. This was exacerbated by the outbreak of the First World War because travel restrictions mostly confined him to Switzerland. Fortunately for him, his introverted personality ensured that he used his isolation creatively:

> *After this break I had with Freud ... I found myself completely isolated. This, however disadvantageous it may have been, had also an advantage for me as an introvert."*
> (McGuire & Shamdasani, 2012, Lecture 3)

He embarked on an inner journey of introspection and a personal "confrontation with the unconscious" which he experienced as a *"creative illness."* As someone with a healing profession, he first had to heal his broken self.

The healing from brokenness is a medical principle that can be traced to the Latin *"Cura te ipsum,"* which means *"Physician, heal thyself."* This expression, which urged physicians to heal themselves before treating patients, was based on the belief that a sick physician is really a patient, who, until cured, is impeded in the act of healing. If you are sick and want to get better, would you go to a sick doctor? No. The same principle holds in psychology. A psychologist needs to find his or her own healing before treating clients.

Imagine spending seven years in isolation—like Jung did—going down a long, dark and lonely tunnel, not knowing when you will see the light at the end. And yet, it is something we have to deal with when life loses its meaning, usually after a great loss of some kind. The 16th-century Spanish monk, St. John of the Cross, called it the *"dark night of the soul."* Through it, we can re-discover the very essence of who we are and undergo a psychological rebirth. In modern society, however, we tend to numb ourselves with medication if there is a psychological crisis. This can sometimes be necessary, but it can also prolong healing and prevent us from arriving at a place of conscious awakening to a new sense of life.

Jung embarked on this inner journey through writing a series of journals named the *Black Books*. He said it was *"my most difficult experiment."* In these journals, he recorded all his inner explorations, dreams, and reflections so that he could somehow objectify and process them. We can only face the content the unconscious throws at us by finding a way to detach ourselves from it. If for example, we are overwhelmed by fear, the best way to deal with the fear is by examining it as if it were an everyday problem like deciding which groceries to buy. The content of Jung's inner journey was not published until this century (2009), as *The Red Book* or *Liber Novus* (Latin for "New Book"). His first words in the book are: *"The way of what is to come.*" With these journals as his instrument, he surrendered himself to his own unconscious and waited for "what was to come."

In Jung's case, one of the things that "was to come," was his work *Psychological Types* (published in 1921, seven years after his break-up with Freud), in which he was able to work through and understand his differences with Freud from a typological perspective. He writes in *Memories, Dreams, Reflections*:

> *This work sprang originally from my need to define the ways in which my outlook differed from Freud's and Adler's. In attempting to answer this question, I came across the problem of types; for it is one's psychological type which from the outset determines and limits a person's judgment. My book, therefore, was an effort to deal with the relationship of the individual to the world, to people and things.*
> (Jung, 1989, Chapter VII: The Work)

But before diving into Jung's typology, it is important to understand something about the purpose of his psychology, which we turn to next.

"creative illness." As someone with a healing profession, he first had to heal his broken self.

The healing from brokenness is a medical principle that can be traced to the Latin *"Cura te ipsum,"* which means *"Physician, heal thyself."* This expression, which urged physicians to heal themselves before treating patients, was based on the belief that a sick physician is really a patient, who, until cured, is impeded in the act of healing. If you are sick and want to get better, would you go to a sick doctor? No. The same principle holds in psychology. A psychologist needs to find his or her own healing before treating clients.

Imagine spending seven years in isolation—like Jung did—going down a long, dark and lonely tunnel, not knowing when you will see the light at the end. And yet, it is something we have to deal with when life loses its meaning, usually after a great loss of some kind. The 16th-century Spanish monk, St. John of the Cross, called it the *"dark night of the soul."* Through it, we can re-discover the very essence of who we are and undergo a psychological rebirth. In modern society, however, we tend to numb ourselves with medication if there is a psychological crisis. This can sometimes be necessary, but it can also prolong healing and prevent us from arriving at a place of conscious awakening to a new sense of life.

Jung embarked on this inner journey through writing a series of journals named the *Black Books*. He said it was *"my most difficult experiment."* In these journals, he recorded all his inner explorations, dreams, and reflections so that he could somehow objectify and process them. We can only face the content the unconscious throws at us by finding a way to detach ourselves from it. If for example, we are overwhelmed by fear, the best way to deal with the fear is by examining it as if it were an everyday problem like deciding which groceries to buy. The content of Jung's inner journey was not published until this century (2009), as *The Red Book* or *Liber Novus* (Latin for "New Book"). His first words in the book are: *"The way of what is to come.*" With these journals as his instrument, he surrendered himself to his own unconscious and waited for "what was to come."

In Jung's case, one of the things that "was to come," was his work *Psychological Types* (published in 1921, seven years after his break-up with Freud), in which he was able to work through and understand his differences with Freud from a typological perspective. He writes in *Memories, Dreams, Reflections*:

This work sprang originally from my need to define the ways in which my outlook differed from Freud's and Adler's. In attempting to answer this question, I came across the problem of types; for it is one's psychological type which from the outset determines and limits a person's judgment. My book, therefore, was an effort to deal with the relationship of the individual to the world, to people and things.
(Jung, 1989, Chapter VII: The Work)

But before diving into Jung's typology, it is important to understand something about the purpose of his psychology, which we turn to next.

CHAPTER 5

THE PURPOSE OF JUNGIAN PSYCHOLOGY

The psyche is the greatest of all cosmic wonders and the "sine qua non" of the world as we know it. It is in the highest degree odd that Western man, with but very few—and ever fewer—exceptions, pays so little regard to this fact.

~ C.G. Jung, CW 8, § 357

What is this "greatest of all cosmic wonders"? The Greek word psyche means "soul," "spirit" or "breath of life." The psyche is the sum of the conscious and unconscious human mind, and psychology is the study of it. Or as Jung wrote:

By psyche, I understand the totality of all psychic processes, both conscious as well as unconscious.
(Jung, CW 6, § 797)

The conscious-unconscious polarity is the great, fundamental polarity in the psyche that encompasses all other polarities. To understand this polarity better, let us have a closer look at the roles these separate but interacting systems play in Jungian psychology.

Consciousness
Consciousness is the domain of the ego, the part of us that is aware of our thoughts and actions, of our inner world as well as the world around us. It organizes our perception, our memories and it takes the decisions that we as individuals must make. As such it is the center of consciousness and the seat of our identity. To give an idea of the relative magnitude of each, Jung described the ego as a cork and the unconscious as the ocean on which it floats.

The unconscious for Jung has two layers, a personal one and a collective one:

Personal Unconscious
The first layer below ego consciousness is the Personal Unconscious, and it contains all the experiences and impressions an individual's ego has repressed or forgotten over time. They exist in patterns that are called complexes. A complex is a psychological entity that is emotionally charged and autonomous. It acts on its own when triggered and distorts reality. E.g., money complex, inferiority complex, mother complex, father complex, etc. A parental complex, for example, is the result of the experiences with the personal parent and can be both positive (e.g., the nourishing parent) and negative (e.g., the critical parent).

Because these complexes are emotionally charged and unconscious, they can act out without conscious control and cause havoc. When triggered they tend to distort reality and cause a reaction that might have been proportionate at the time the complex was formed but is now out of proportion. It is only through awareness that the ego gets a grip on them, but only if the ego has enough willpower to detach from them. In some psychological schools, these complexes are called "subpersonalities."

Collective Unconscious

The second and deepest layer is the Collective Unconscious, and it contains the "blueprints of the basic human qualities we all share" (Johnson, 2000, Ch. 5). It contains the powerful universal images, forces, ideas, instincts, thought patterns and concepts called "archetypes" that characterize human existence. They too can emerge in consciousness in either productive or destructive ways. An archetype is like a complex, except that it is collective, not personal. This means there is a Father Archetype, a Mother Archetype, but also a Warrior Archetype, a King Archetype and so on. The fact that it is collective explains why the same phenomena can manifest independently of each other in different parts of the world.

Relationship between Consciousness and the Unconscious

The language of the unconscious is symbolic; it uses images, metaphors, and stories to communicate its content to consciousness. In Marketing, for example, images are used to tap into our unconscious hopes and fears very effectively. Jung observed that a vital dynamic between consciousness and the unconscious is that the unconscious always seeks to compensate for and balance the conscious ego position and that in this sense the psyche is "self-regulating."

Jung called his psychology "analytical psychology" because it is fundamentally concerned with helping the ego understand and process the signals from the personal and collective unconscious about how to lead a more balanced and purposeful life.

What is the Purpose of Humankind?

In an interview with *Cosmopolitan Magazine* in 1934, Jung said:

What nature asks of the apple tree is that it shall bring forth apples. And of the pear tree that it shall bring forth pears. Nature wants me to be simply

man, a man conscious of what I am, and of what I am doing.
(McGuire & Hull, 1987, p. 75)

So, as apple trees bring forth apples, humankind brings forth consciousness of *"what I am and what I am doing."* Jung called this process of becoming who you are as an individual and experiencing meaning, purpose, and growth the *individuation process*.

It is for the purpose of *individuation* that Jung emphasized the adage, *"Know Thyself."* It is only when you know yourself that you can navigate life. A professor at a university may have vast knowledge, but what mattered to Jung is how well you know *yourself*.

This is a bit of a challenge for us as a culture. We are so extraverted in the United States that we spend relatively little time on self-reflection. We do not find it in a standard high school curriculum, for example. And yet it is perhaps the most worthwhile undertaking of a lifetime. Or, as the Greek philosopher Socrates put it, "The unexamined life is not worth living." In other words, the examined life is the one worth living. Jung goes as far as to say:

Every advance, every conceptual achievement of mankind, has been connected with an advance in self-awareness.
(Jung, CW 8, § 523)

When we do not take the time to reflect on and examine our lives, what will tend to happen is that we become like the man:

…who leans over his neighbor's fence and says to him: "Look, there is a weed. And over there is another one. And why don't you hoe the rows deeper? And why don't you tie up the vines?" And all the while, his own garden, behind him, is full of weeds.
(Jung, 1987, p. 75)

Jung called the part of our "garden" that we do not attend to and is full of "weeds" *the Shadow*, and he felt it was important to get to know and take ownership of this part of ourselves so that we can attend to our "garden."

Shadow and Individuation

There is no individuation possible without facing and integrating the Shadow. The expression "A water lily grows in the mud" exists in many cultures. It implies that we grow out of darkness into the light, very much like a lily grows from the mud at the bottom of a lake or canal and surfaces to blossom. We are all like lilies trying to grow to the surface and bloom, and we can only do so if we are firmly rooted in the mud, taking responsibility for and owning our Shadow. Robert Johnson, the author of *Owning Your Own Shadow*, says about this process:

> *...our own Shadow, that dumping ground for all those Shadow characteristics of our personality that we disown... is extremely valuable... To honor and accept one's own Shadow is a profound spiritual discipline. It is whole-making and thus holy, the most important experience of a lifetime.*
> (Johnson, 1993, ix)

Whenever you find yourself in an existential crisis or faced with an impossible challenge, the Shadow can come to your aid by revealing an important truth and energizing consciousness. For instance, you are fired from your job, and years later you realize that it was the best thing that could have happened to you because it opened a new source of life.

In sports teams I have worked with, it was always the integration of the hidden, repressed aspect of a team's personality that had to be integrated to create a truly strong and balanced whole that would be able to win a championship. It was through the integration of the Shadow that the Dutch Olympic team I worked with was able to advance to a higher level of performance that resulted in the ultimate achievement in sports: an Olympic gold medal.

No matter how smart or fast the Ego is, the Shadow will always catch up and demand integration. Jung called this process "enantiodromia," a term he adopted from the ancient Greek philosopher Heraclitus which means "running in opposite direction" (enantios – opposite and dromos – running course). It is like the swing of a pendulum, only psychologically:

> *I use the term enantiodromia for the emergence of the unconscious opposite in the course of time. This characteristic phenomenon practically always occurs when an extreme, one-sided tendency dominates conscious life; in time an equally powerful counter position is built up, which first inhibits the conscious performance and subsequently breaks through the conscious control.*
> (Jung, CW 6, § 709)

The challenge for the ego is to avoid a one-sided approach to life, so the pendulum does not build up too much momentum. The Shadow contains an enormous amount of unconscious energy that can be used to energize life. This is where you find all the polarities, like good-evil, warm-cold, bold-shy, happy-sad. To channel this energy into consciousness, we need a strong ego, an ego that contemplates these qualities without identifying with them or rejecting them. Because the latter inevitably leads to a process whereby we "act out" our unconscious darkness and harm our fellow human beings as well as ourselves.

Ego and Shadow

For Jung, the ego is the "center of consciousness." It is the part of the personality that makes decisions and directs life. It is an agent for self-determination and, as such is crucial for a healthy and unique psychological development. Jungian analyst Murray Stein writes in *Jung's Map of the Soul* (1998):

The ego is what sets humans apart from other creatures of nature who also possess consciousness; it also sets the individual human being apart from other human beings. It is the individualizing agent in human consciousness.
(Chapter 1: The Relation of Ego to Consciousness)

The Shadow is always present, just not consciously. It is responsible for the feelings, thoughts and actions we are not aware of. We act it out and then ask ourselves, "Was that me?" For instance, someone is angered by something but takes this anger out on someone else to discharge the anger and dissipate it. But this causes the other to become angry and lash out, which only perpetuates the cycle. The cycle of violence only stops through consciousness, through an inner exploration and transformation of the unconscious content.

Jung emphasized that the ego is the moral center of the personality. The ego decides how to interact with the Shadow, how to face the contents of its own neglected garden, what to do with it, and how to tend it. Jung saw this as a moral responsibility and challenge:

The Shadow is a moral problem that challenges the whole ego-personality, for no one can become conscious of the Shadow without considerable moral effort. To become conscious of it involves recognizing the dark aspects of the personality as present and real.
(Jung, CW 9ii, § 14)

In Jungian psychology, the ego has an almost heroic role. It is the valve that connects the unconscious with consciousness; it is the agent whose main task is to balance the polarities in the psyche and use sound moral judgment to do so. How can the ego face this challenge?

When only one side of a polarity is acknowledged, the other retreats into the Shadow, waiting for and seeking redemption into consciousness. In everyday life, the Shadow is what trips you up and disturbs you in its attempts to break through to your consciousness. When this occurs, the best thing to do is to try to listen to its message without judgment, shame, or blame. The clue that your own Shadow is involved is revealed by the extent to which you are upset. Should you find yourself confronted by someone you do not like, or fall out with a colleague or your spouse, then these are the moments to examine your unconscious thoughts and see what they have to say about you, not the other.

Let us say you have a colleague or business partner with whom you enjoy working. If you pay attention, you may notice that feelings of envy or fear of betrayal and abandonment lurk in your unconscious. If you are unaware of this, the chances are that you will act out your envy by trying to take something from that person, or you might abandon them to preempt being abandoned yourself.

The way to deal with these unconscious impulses is to reverse engineer them. It starts with awareness of what you are thinking, doing, feeling. When you feel envious of someone, you can be sure that the unconscious is giving you a hint of something you are missing and want to have in your life. It is an excellent opportunity to become conscious of what that is. If you feel envious of your neighbors' house, for example, ask yourself what the qualities of their house are that you envy so much. Because that reveals something about what you value and the house you would like to create for yourself. Or if you are afraid of being betrayed or abandoned by someone, ask yourself: Where am I not being true to myself? How am I abandoning my values?

Perhaps a more direct example is this: do you feel upset when someone is unkind, direct and blunt? Ask yourself: have I suppressed my own directness and how could I benefit from being more direct? Or, you feel that person is too soft, touchy-feely and "Kumbaya"? Ask yourself: where have I abandoned my vulnerable side, which longs for connection?

Jung could not have put it better when he wrote:

That I feed the beggar, that I forgive an insult, that I love my enemy in the name of Christ - all these are undoubtedly great virtues. But what if I should discover that the least among them all, the poorest of all beggars, the most impudent of all offenders, yea the very fiend himself - that these are within me, and that I myself stand in need of my own kindness, that I myself am the enemy who must be loved in the name of Christ - what then?
(Jung, CW 10, § 520)

Jung considered it the moral and ethical responsibility of the ego to fully face all aspects of oneself, including the Shadow, with acceptance and love. It is the conscious ego that can stop us from acting out from our Shadow. And I know of no more practical way to start this process, than by examining the polarities of one's personality.

The Great Human Challenge

Individuation can be postponed but not avoided altogether. The psychological and physical damage caused by doing so is too great. Avoidance leads to neurosis and from there to strife, from small family feuds to major global conflicts. We live in a time when mental illness affects one in five adults in the U.S. (based on statistics provided by the National Alliance on Mental Illness). It is important that we develop more psychological skills in society.

It is part of being human to be both conscious and unconscious, so we all suffer from this condition and from the consequences of unconscious decisions. At the same time, if we can become more conscious and take responsibility for our own emotions in a conflict, unconscious suffering and destruction can be replaced by psychological growth and a sense of peace, even happiness. There is a lot at stake. On a global level, Jung was very concerned about wars and saw a lack of consciousness mirrored in global conflicts. In the 1934 *Cosmopolitan Magazine* interview Jung talked about the psychology of war:

Tell me, what is the most destructive thing you know of? Fire, earthquake, volcanic eruptions, floods, diseases... What about World War? Ah yes! But, do explosives make themselves? Do they declare war? Do they bring men with them? It is the psyche of man that makes wars. Not his consciousness... his unconscious which contains all the inherited savagery as well as spiritual strivings of the race, says to him, "Now it is time to kill and destroy." And he does it. No cosmic power on earth ever destroyed ten million men, but man's psyche did, and it can do it again.
(McGuire & Hull, 1987, p. 73)

As those of us who now live in the 21st century know, "man's psyche did do it again." The Second World War erupted five years after this interview and resulted in 60 million casualties worldwide. His concern with global destruction is just as relevant today as it was back then. Jung stressed the importance of psychology to avert such a tragedy:

We need more psychology. We need more understanding of human nature. Because... man... is the great danger, and we are pitifully unaware of it... His psyche should be studied because we are the origin of all coming evil.
(McGuire & Hull, 1987, p. 436)

In summary, the purpose of Jungian psychology is to develop a consciousness that is both willing to uncover and live its highest purpose as well as reveal its darkest and most negative impulses, and make the decision not to act on them, but confront and transform them. He called this process *Individuation*.

How should we start this process? Jungian typology is a human compass for this journey of self-discovery. It is with reason that he called the functions of the personality "functions of consciousness." In other words, it is through the functions of the personality that we can know ourselves and know the world.

In the next chapter, we will delve into his work on typology and explore it as a practical and concrete framework for self-reflection and consciousness.

Chapter 6

Jungian Typology 101

> *In my practical medical work, I have long been struck by the fact that besides the many individual differences in human psychology there are also typical differences.*
>
> ~ C.G. Jung, CW 6, § 1

Any experience you have is structured by the mind, specifically by the part we call the personality. It structures information, decisions, and actions. That is why it is said that reality is not in front of your eyes but behind them. The typical way in which a mind processes information is called a personality type. A typology is a system or model that categorizes personality types. The system presented by Carl Jung in *Psychological Types* is widely referred to as "Jungian Typology."

Jung once said in an interview: *"Type is nothing static."* What he meant was that you cannot use it to put people (or yourself) in a box. Instead, it is a powerful framework for understanding the polarities of the personality, ours and others. We can use it to become aware of and facilitate a dynamic interaction between their poles. With the goal of achieving a healthy balance, not something "static."

Typology is a powerful way to discover a person's individuality and find ways to optimize human understanding, collaboration, and development. Since it is so powerful and attractive to many people, it is important to list some ethical considerations that apply to its use:

- Every person is unique and uses their personality in their own, unique way.
- An individual, not their personality, is in charge of their life.
- You can do anything you set your mind to.
- A self-assessment of the personality is per definition subjective.
- It is up to the individual to recognize their best fit or true type. No "test" can do that for you.
- Type cannot be used as a box, label, or as an excuse.
- Intelligence and skills cannot be inferred from a personality type.
- There has never been nor probably will there ever be a definitive and final theory of the personality. Theories progress and different theories can complement each other.

With this understanding, let us turn to Jung's theory of the personality.

Jungian Polarities of the Personality

Jung modeled his insights into the typical differences between people into a framework that distinguish three polarities (or pairs of opposite poles) in the personality. These polarities are tools, faculties and types of intelligence everyone has access to. Even though many are not aware of how they are using them or how powerful they are, these deeply human faculties are always there, ready to be accessed. Like all of life, the personality is made up of polarities, because is the tension between opposites that creates life.

Each polarity has a specific task:
- Gathering information (called "Perceiving")
- Making decisions (called "Judging")
- Connecting our inner and outer world (called "Attitude")

Of these polarities Jung said:

I have found from experience that the basic psychological functions, that is, functions which are both genuinely as well as essentially differentiated from other functions, there exist Thinking, Feeling, Sensation, and Intuition. If one of these functions habitually prevails, a corresponding type results. Every one of these types can moreover be introverted or extraverted in attitude.
(Jung, CW 6, § 7)

The table below describes the three polarity pairs and their specific tasks:

Task	Polarities	
Perceiving Functions *Gathering information*	**Sensation (S)** *Facts*	**Intuition (N)** *Imagination*
Judging Functions *Making decisions*	**Thinking (T)** *Causality and logic*	**Feeling (F)** *People and relationships*
Attitude *Connecting inner and outer world*	**Introversion (I)** *Reflection*	**Extraversion (E)** *(Inter)action*

It is important to bear the following in mind:
- All three polarities are always present in us.
- There are no right or wrong, good or bad, useful or useless polarities.
- We tend to favor and rely on individual poles within the polarities more than others. This is called *Preference*.

Example of Everyday Use of the Functions and Attitudes

Let's take a cup as a simple example of how these polarities operate in our personality. When we hold a cup in our hands, *Sensation* tells us that there is a physical object with a particular shape. *Thinking* tells us the object is a cup. *Feeling* tells us whether we like it, whether it is agreeable or not. And *Intuition* tells us the potential of the cup, what we can do with it. With our *Introversion*, we reflect on the cup, and with our *Extraversion*, we interact with it, we use it.

Color Associations with the Four Functions

Jung discovered in his research and work with his clients that there was a color pattern associated with the four functions:

> *The four colours attributed to the functions are based on certain feeling values. Feeling is red, this is connected with blood and fire, with passion and love which is supposed to be warm and glowing. Sensation is green, this is connected with the earth and perceiving reality. Thinking is white, or blue, cold like snow and Intuition is gold or yellow because it is felt to shine and radiate.*
> (C. G. Jung, Modern Psychology: ETH Lectures, Volume 4)

The four primary colors can be used as just another way to reference the functions. Sensation, for example, can be referred to as "Green Sensation," or the "Green color of the personality," or just "Green." Time will tell what works and communicates best, the point is that the colors offer a useful, practical metaphor for the functions. See for clarification the figure on the next page of the function polarities and their colors.

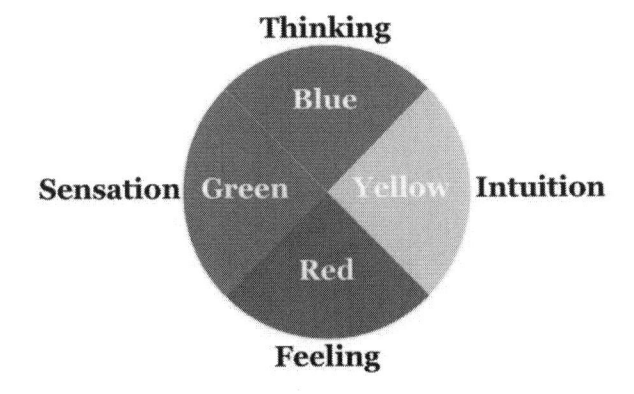

Next, what are these functions and how do they interact with each other? We will first look at the *Perceiving* functions (Sensation and Intuition), then the *Judging* functions (Thinking and Feeling) and finally at the *Attitudes* (Introversion and Extraversion).

Perceiving: Sensation vs. Intuition

Sensation (S) gathers information through the five senses: sight, smell, taste, touch, and hearing. It perceives the tangible reality in the here-and-now, it is interested in knowing the facts and details, and in gathering real, verifiable data. It needs to see the "small picture" before seeing the "big picture." When looking at a forest, it sees individual trees before seeing the forest.

Intuition (N) uses the "sixth sense" to gather information. It sees beyond the facts to the things that exist outside of tangible reality. Like ideas, concepts, potentials, and dreams. It needs to see the "big picture" before it can focus on the "small picture." It sees the forest before it sees the individual trees.

Once, in the company of a friend, I was admiring the vast, beautiful ocean as the sun sank below the horizon when he turned to me and asked, *"Do you see that boat there? I wonder who is on it, where they came from and where they're going?"* I was focused on the "forest," he on an individual "tree."

The many differences in perception are summarized in the table below. This is an oversimplification, but a useful one to understand the differences between these functions. Review this table both vertically and horizontally. See which mode of perception you prefer.

Sensation	*Intuition*
5 Senses	6th Sense
Hard facts	Imagination
Specific details	Big picture
Precise	General
Practical and hands-on	Conceptual and original
Tangible reality	Possibilities
Present and past	Future
Tradition	Change
Proven	Hypothetical
Concrete	Symbolic
Conventional	Original
Experience	Belief or Hunch
Data	Meaning
Reality	Potential

Let's take a moment to look at specific differences in this table. It says that Sensation focuses on the present and the past, and Intuition on the future. I have noticed how Sensation is comfortable with actual events both present and in the past. But the events that might occur in the future are a cause for concern; after all, they are not yet tangible, they are still a "big unknown." So, what Sensation does is try to get all the "future facts" straight. What is going to happen? What will we do once we are there? Exactly when are we going to go there? And if a past experience that is relevant to the current or future situation comes to mind, it is immediately referenced. Once Sensation knows what lies ahead and can reference past experiences, there is a relief. If it cannot, there is anxiety and stress.

Intuition, on the other hand, is stressed by detailed planning, to which it is simply impossible to adhere. The future is something that is created, not planned! So, Intuition moves into the future by dreaming it, by being open to and recognizing possibilities that it wants to actualize. What happened in the past lies in the past, how can it be relevant today? But Sensation works very differently. If Sensation goes to a restaurant twice a month and orders the same dish, it knows exactly what the difference in taste is. And it enjoys comparing notes between the two.

When it comes to change, Sensation is good at handling practical change. If it must eat an elephant, it does so one bite at a time. Intuition will try to devour the elephant in a single mouthful and choke. But creating something really new? Trailblazing unknown territory? With an uncanny prescience, Intuition will see where to go and what to avoid because of impending danger.

Although these perceptions can be worlds apart, they come together every day. The poles must harmonize. For example, what if we want to build a house? We will mostly employ Sensation to use tools and other tangible resources to assemble the building. But we will also need Intuition to imagine the house and design it on paper. While building it, we will most probably encounter problems for which there are no standard solutions and for which we will need our Intuition to envisage the options.

There is a funny anecdote about Sensation and Intuition that is worth sharing here. It is from Joseph Wheelwright, one of Jung's students and the founder of the C.G. Jung Institute of San Francisco. In it, he relates an experience he had during his medical training in London:

There was a man named Lord Horder on the staff of St. Bartholomew's Hospital, who was a brilliant diagnostician and physician—he was the King's physician, actually. He conducted weekly rounds... and they were magnificent performances. One day... he stopped in front of a bed, and said, "Wheelwright, have a look at that chap." I went over, and there was this man, lying in bed. I did what seemed the most sensible thing to do. I looked out the window for some time, but nothing came to me. And then I had a go at the ceiling—and that did it! It came very clear; there was no doubt in my mind, and I turned to him with a broad smile and said, "Lord Horder, sir, this man is suffering from pulmonary tuberculosis." I've never seen a man go so puce more quickly. He said, "As a matter of fact, he IS suffering from pulmonary tuberculosis. How you ever knew it, God only knows. But that is absolutely unimportant. Do you know that doctors have methods they have developed... I see a thing sticking out of your pocket; I believe it's called a stethoscope. You could have put it on his chest, and if you were thoughtful, you would warm it up first on the palms of your hand. And you would say to him, 'My dear chap, say after me, ninety-nine.' Did you? No. Did you use your voice? You know, you might have. We do that quite often. You could have said, 'What brings you here, my good man?'"

I felt very crushed, because I thought I'm really not going to be a smash hit as a doctor...

(Wheelwright, 1973, p. 14)

This humorous discourse shows the difference and misunderstanding between Sensation and Intuition. They can reach the same conclusion but do so very differently. Sensation observes and looks for factual evidence, then records it. Intuition "sniffs" around until there is a certain "click," which just feels "right."

Power of Sensation-Intuition Polarity: New Beginnings

The power of this polarity is that it creates new life, it brings new ideas to fruition. It is a combination of practical action (Sensation) inspired by new ideas and concepts (Intuition). Where Sensation sees reality, Intuition sees potentiality. And when these two come together, new life is born.

I believe it was Edison who said, *"Vision without execution is merely hallucination."* In typological terms, that is like saying that Intuition without Sensation is a hallucination, which is probably psychologically fairly accurate. But a Japanese proverb says it better: *"Vision without action is a daydream. Action without vision is a nightmare."* And then Nelson Mandela adds the crowning element: *"But vision with action can change the world."* That accurately describes the creative tension between Sensation and Intuition as functions of consciousness.

A good example of this is the collaboration between Steve Wozniak and Steve Jobs at Apple Computers. Jobs saw the future of personal computing with his Intuition and understood what a personal computer would be able to do. Wozniak was the brilliant engineer who used Sensation to build the hardware, circuit board, and operating system for the first Apple computer in 1976.

Everyone uses both functions. At the same time, most of us tend to focus, trust and rely on one more than another.

Judging: Thinking vs. Feeling

We appraise, organize, and act on the information we receive with the Blue Thinking (T) and Red Feeling (F) functions. Thinking (T) tends to organize impressions logically in a manner that is impersonal, objective, and task-oriented. Thinking provides direction and leads the way towards achievements. It analyzes information to find the cause and effect, consistency, and logical order of things. The impact a decision has on another person is just another data point, not a criterion in itself. The direction and achievement are what matter most. A decision is made primarily from the head, not the heart.

Feeling (F), on the other hand, likes to organize impressions through a personal and more subjective value judgment, such as a like or a dislike. It looks at information from the perspective of care for personal values, needs, and relationships. It is personal and people-oriented, whereas Thinking is more impersonal and task-oriented. The impact a decision has on another person is NOT just another data point; it is a criterion in itself. Feeling makes decisions from the heart, whereas Thinking makes them from the head. There is a pun by the 17th-century French philosopher Blaise Pascal which describes the difference between the Thinking and Feeling functions as follows: *The heart has its reasons of which reason knows nothing.*

In organizations or teams, one of the ways the difference between these functions becomes prevalent is when it comes to firing someone. For a manager with a Thinking preference, this is primarily a logical task that needs to be executed and is relatively easy to do. Strictly speaking, a person is a resource for the Thinking function. And when they have to be replaced, well... they have to be replaced. Objectively speaking, Thinking is right.

For Feeling, this is close to impossible because there is a personal connection. It feels a responsibility to maintain that relationship with loyalty and commitment. In fact, Feeling would rather sacrifice his or her job to save someone else's. Take a coach of a sports team with a strong Feeling preference, for example. He or she will find it very hard to bench a player, harder even to cut that player from the team.

The many differences in decision-making are summarized in the table below. This too is an oversimplification, but it helps us to understand the differences between these functions. This table should be reviewed both vertically and horizontally. See if you can identify which mode of perception you prefer.

Thinking	Feeling
Logical	Personal
Head	Heart
Objective	Subjective
Analysis	Relationship
Problems	Needs
Cause-Effect	Value
Challenging	Supporting
Reason	Empathy
Critical	Accepting
Tough	Tender
Argument	Appreciation
Discussion	Harmony
Firm	Adaptable
Cool	Warm
Criteria	Care
Transaction	Relation
Intellectual	Aesthetical
How?	Who?

Although these ways of making decisions can be worlds apart, they come together every day. If we revisit the example of building a house, we will use our Thinking function to put together the house logically and efficiently. But we will also need Feeling because the Feeling function can tell us what makes a house useful, beautiful and an enjoyable place to be.

Power of the Thinking-Feeling Polarity: Setting Norms for Development

It is through this polarity that the new life generated by the Sensation-Intuition polarity is developed, cultivated and refined in order to have an impact. For example, it is the combination of Science (Thinking) and Art (Feeling) that provides knowledge in concert with relatedness and beauty. And each has very different values and norms. Thinking prefers norms that are logically consistent, mechanistic and transactional. Feeling prefers norms based on a personal connection, appreciation and relationship. They are both necessary, and any organization needs to have enough of both to not lose balance. If this balance is maintained carefully, astonishing results are possible.

Let's look at Apple again. After Steve Jobs and Steve Wozniak created the first personal computer, Jobs paired up with designer Jonathan Ive to create products like the iMac, iPhone, and iPad. These products are both technically sound (Thinking) and works of art (Feeling). Most Apple products are known for their combination of aesthetic and functional qualities. They are not just products that are functional; they are objects that are cherished and loved.

Everyone uses both functions. At the same time, most of us tend to focus, trust and rely on one more than another.

Connecting Inner and Outer Worlds: Introversion vs. Extraversion

Let's look for a moment at the etymological origins of these words. "Introversion" comes from the Latin *"intro"* (inward) and *"vertere"* (to turn), which, compounded, mean a turning inwards. Similarly, "extraversion" comes from the Latin *"extra"* (outward) and *"vertere"* (to turn), i.e., a turning outwards. Introversion stands for contraction and rooting within one's self. Extraversion stands for expansion and reaching outside one's self. Introversion is the centripetal force of the personality, extraversion the centrifugal.

Here we will use the metaphor of the forest again. In fall and winter, the forest introverts and the energy withdraws to the roots below the ground. In spring and summer, the forest extraverts and the energy goes upward and outwards to the branches and leaves.

Introversion and extraversion are about the movement of psychic energy, like exhaling (E) and inhaling (I). We all introvert and extravert for longer or shorter periods of time. However, in about 1/3 of the population one or the other is dominant. In the analogy of breathing in and breathing out, an extraverted preference is equivalent to taking a short breath in followed by a long breath out. Introversion prefers to reflect and process internally. Extraversion prefers to act and process externally.

For instance, an extravert will seek to gain an understanding of something by discussing it. He or she will seek this thought process in the outside world. An introvert will want to go inside and process it internally first. I remember having a meeting to discuss a certain policy decision with a board of advisors. As an extravert, I enjoyed interacting with others, and it helped me see our advisors' different points of view. My colleague who was more introverted and self-reliant did not. His response was "Why do we need this? We can make this decision on our own!" As can be seen from this example, both the introverted and extraverted viewpoint must be allowed the space to reach a balanced point of view. Personally, after hearing different points of view, I need my introverted side to arrive at my own opinion.

The introverted attitude feels most alive when absorbed in the inner world. It is there that it is active. By listening and reflecting it produces a depth and quality of content that the extraverted attitude cannot achieve. Introverted athletes often reach high-performance levels because of their ability to practice alone and reflect on the game. In teams that do not function well, they are often the ones who can identify the cause. They know the value of introspection but are not always valued for it. When the gems they hold inside are appreciated by and shared with the team, they always provide new momentum.

The extraverted attitude feels most alive when interacting with the outer world. Its activity is visible to everyone, and it enjoys a rich, busy environment where it can act as a "mover and shaker." In sports teams, the extraverted players have a high action radius and communicate loud and clear, but run the risk of losing focus and prematurely exhausting themselves.

In the 20th century, education and business were structured to favor the extravert. Large corporations with large offices, big schools, and classrooms all created a very stimulating environment for the extraverted attitude. The Internet and computer technology are shifting this to the benefit of the introvert. An education can be completed or a business created from the solitude of a computer screen. This shift is enormously valuable when adopted properly by society. It means the introverted and extraverted attitude can become truly "connected."

Susan Cain is an insightful speaker and author dedicated to unlocking the power of introversion. The following is helpful for extraversion in understanding introversion:

> *The next time you see a person with a composed face and a soft voice, remember that inside her mind she might be solving an equation, composing a sonnet, designing a hat. She might, that is, be deploying the power of quiet.*
> (Cain, 2012, Conclusion)

Typical words that tend to be associated with the attitudes of introversion-extraversion are listed below. This chart is simplified to help identify the differences between these attitudes.

Introversion	Extraversion
Reflective	(Inter)active
Calm	Busy
Reserved	Outgoing
Listen	Talk
Reflect, act later	Act, reflect later
Cautious	Daring
Depth	Breadth
Private	Open
Observe	Act
Wait	Initiate

Research indicates that most people are ambiverts in that they combine these attitudes quite readily. This has been my experience as well, yet I have also found that under stress most ambiverts prefer one mode to the other.

I have a friend who is an entrepreneur who can easily switch between his introverted and extraverted mode. What is interesting though is that he prefers to work alone and completely rejects the idea of having an office where he would meet co-workers every day. He also has no desire to expand his company. This shows his deeper preference for introversion. An extravert would welcome the opportunity to have an office and meet co-workers there and would like to create a company that has a significant impact on the outer world.

Another example that comes to mind is when I was on an outing with a friend. At one point, he sat down on a couch. Since I was eager to do something (my extraverted attitude), I asked him what he wanted to do. To which he answered, "I don't know, I'm going to sit here and think about it."

Nothing is what it seems though, and you cannot assume that type is always a good predictor of behavior. Or as Jung said, "Type is nothing static." In the following excerpt, Jung gives a humorous example of how within the same person the introverted attitude can flip into the extraverted attitude and vice versa. As the story shows, this can lead to unexpected outcomes.

> *Let us suppose two youths rambling in the country come upon a fine castle; both want to see inside it. The introvert says, "I'd like to know what it's like inside." The extravert answers, "Right, let's go in," and makes for the gateway. The introvert draws back — "Perhaps we aren't allowed in," says he, with visions of policemen, fines, and fierce dogs in the background. Whereupon the extravert answers, "Well, we can ask. They'll let us in all right" — with visions of kindly old watchmen, hospitable seigneurs, and the possibility of romantic adventures. On the strength of extraverted optimism, they at length find themselves in the castle. But now comes the dénouement. The castle has been rebuilt inside, and contains nothing but a couple of rooms with a collection of old manuscripts. As it happens, old manuscripts are the chief joy of the introverted youth. Hardly has he caught sight of them than he becomes as one transformed. He loses himself in contemplation of the treasures, uttering cries of enthusiasm... But meanwhile the spirits of the extraverted youth are ebbing lower and lower. His face grows longer and he begins to yawn. No kindly watchmen are forthcoming here, no knightly hospitality, not a trace of romantic adventure — only a castle made over into a museum... While the enthusiasm of the one rises, the spirits of the other fall, the castle bores him, the manuscripts remind him of a library, library is associated with university, university with studies and menacing examinations. Gradually a veil of gloom descends over the once so interesting and enticing castle. The object becomes negative. "Isn't it marvelous," cries the introvert, "to have stumbled on this wonderful collection?" "The place bores me to extinction," replies the other with undisguised ill humour. This annoys the introvert, who secretly vows never again to go rambling with an extravert. The latter is annoyed with the other's annoyance, and he thinks to himself that he always knew the fellow was an inconsiderate egotist*

who would, in his own selfish interest, waste all the lovely spring day that could be enjoyed so much better out of doors.
(Jung, CW 7i, § 81)

So what happened here? This example is a good illustration how we can come into the grip of our opposite function or attitude. The more introverted youth all of a sudden finds his extraversion aroused and cannot let go of this castle. The extravert is "bored to extinction" by the introversion he experiences.

This example shows why it is so important to understand the dynamic of type and how easily we can flip into our shadow side without being aware of it. If the two youths of the story had been aware of their types, they could have handled the situation much better, given each other space to do their own thing. After all, they did help each other. The extravert helped the introvert to enter the castle. There the introvert found things that could be of value to others and could be brought into the world by the extravert.

Type is About Preference

When Jung said that everyone is different, but some differences are typical, he was talking about preference. Preference is a combination of nature and nurture and one way to understand it is by doing the following exercise.

Cross your arms in front of you. Which arm is on top? Your right or left? I bet that if you did this, you'd find that nine times out of ten the same arm would be on top. Does this mean you don't have the ability to do it the other way around? No, it just isn't your preference. Writing with your right instead of your left hand is also a preference. This does not mean you couldn't write with your left hand. In fact, some people have taught themselves to do just that.

It is the same with the personality. Although we can access and use all three polarity pairs, we do have a preference. And it is our preference that tends to be the best developed and therefore differentiated. It becomes different through development and growth. That is also the advantage having a preference: it develops the preferred function to a high degree. The disadvantage is that it can act as a filter that blocks the other functions. The preferred way becomes the "best way" to accomplish something.

A good method of discerning which poles of a polarity you prefer are to see how much energy it takes to use that function or attitude. Is it easy and natural? Does it energize you? Are you drawn to it? Or does it tend to be a struggle, does it drain you of energy?

A person with an introverted attitude needs some time alone, needs to be able to "go inside" regularly to reflect and focus. Interacting with the outer world can be cumbersome and tiring. At work, this is the person who likes to sit behind their desk and focus, with as few interruptions as possible. A more extraverted person likes to interact with others, or attend meetings, presentations, or lunches. And perhaps you have noticed that extraverts tend to communicate with a somewhat louder voice?

Jung made an important observation concerning preference and choosing between the four functions (S/N/T/F):

- The most preferred and the least preferred are usually opposites
- The two in between serve and aid the most preferred function

Jung states this clearly in Psychological Types:

Experience shows that the secondary function is always one whose nature is different from, though not antagonistic to, the primary function: Thus,

Thinking, as the primary function, can readily pair with Intuition as the auxiliary, or indeed equally well with Sensation, but...never with Feeling.
(Jung, CW 6, § 668)

Closer investigation shows with great regularity that, besides the most differentiated function, another, less differentiated function of secondary importance is invariably present in consciousness and exerts a co-determining influence.
(Jung, CW 6, § 666)

These observations resulted in a naming convention for the order in which the four functions interact in the personality, which is useful and important to understand and apply:

1. ***Dominant function*** (used and relied upon most)
2. ***Auxiliary function*** (used and relied upon next)
3. ***Tertiary function*** (used occasionally)
4. ***Inferior function*** (used more selectively and with little or even no conscious control)

The four functions are like entrances to the personality, and determining which one is dominant (or the "main entrance") is the first step to understanding one's type. The next step is to determine which one is auxiliary (the "side entrance"). Together they constitute the "primary function pair" in the personality.

The tertiary function (the "other side entrance") is not used as often. The inferior function (the "back door") is an essential door to have, although there are usually problems with it (as it is either stuck or a bit squeaky, to say the least). The term "inferior" is somewhat misleading though because besides being squeaky, it also is the function of consciousness which brings new insights and (leads to) personal growth. It is the "young fool" in our personality that does the thing that is most needed. It is like the young Luke Skywalker in *Star Wars* who saves the Galaxy.

Carl Jung analyzed his own personality during an interview conducted in 1959 by John Freeman for the wonderful BBC television series, *Face to Face*:

Freeman: *Have you concluded what psychological type you are yourself?*

Jung: *Naturally, I have devoted a great deal of attention to that painful question.*

Freeman: *And reached a conclusion?*

Jung: *Well, you see, type is nothing static, it changes in the course of life. But I most certainly was characterized by Thinking. I always thought, from early childhood on. I had a great deal of Intuition, too. And I had a definite difficulty with Feeling. And my relation to reality was not particularly brilliant. I was often at variance with the reality of things. Now that gives you all the necessary data for diagnosis.*

What Jung is saying here is that Thinking is his strongest, and therefore dominant function. It is closely followed by Intuition, his auxiliary function. His greatest difficulty is with Feeling, so that is his inferior function. And although his Sensation function is not brilliant, it is present but only as his tertiary function. If Jung's self-analysis is correct, this is the order of preference for his four functions:
   1. Thinking (T)
   2. Intuition (N)
   3. Sensation (S)
   4. Feeling (F)

There is an exercise you can do to determine the order in which you use functions. In the table below mark the words that apply and appeal most to you. Then count how many words you marked in each column. See which of the functions has the highest score, which is second, third, and fourth.

Perceiving		Judging	
Sensation	**Intuition**	**Thinking**	**Feeling**
Factual	Imaginative	Logical	Personal
5 Senses	6th Sense	Head	Heart
Precise	General	Objective	Subjective
Data	Meaning	Analysis	Relationship
Details	Ideas	Problems	Needs
Present	Future	Cause-effect	Value
Proven	Hypothetical	Challenging	Supporting
Concrete	Symbolic	Reason	Empathy
Traditional	Original	Critical	Accepting
Safe	Risky	Tough	Tender
Routine	Variety	Argument	Appreciation
Actuality	Possibility	Discussion	Harmony
Practical	Abstract	Firm	Adaptable
Form	Content	Cool	Warm
Experience	Belief	Criteria	Care
Sensible	Speculative	Intellectual	Aesthetical
What?	Why?	How?	Who?

Tally your counts here:
Sensation: _____
Intuition: _____
Thinking: _____
Feeling: _____

Remember, the function that is dominant is determined as much by your highest as by your lowest score. If for instance, you have high counts for both Thinking and Intuition, with Intuition slightly higher. Which one is dominant? If your lowest count is for Feeling, then your Thinking function will probably be dominant and not

Intuition. Because if Feeling has the lowest count, that probably means it is your inferior function. And the dominant function is always the opposite. Hence Thinking will likely be dominant.

Function-Attitudes

Each function can be expressed in an extraverted or introverted attitude. Extraverted Thinking is action-oriented, introverted Thinking reflection-oriented. Although this is an important distinction and one Carl Jung makes explicitly in *Psychological Types*, my experience is that in general people introvert and extravert the dominant function in their personality quite well. The metaphor I use here is a front door of a house. If I take myself as an example, Intuition is the front door of the house of my personality, and I use it to go in and out of the house. I use it to extravert, and I use it to introvert.

Nature, Nurture, and Behavior

The personality develops through both nature and nurture and is a hugely important factor driving our behavior. It does not, however, have a monopoly on our behavior. Behavior is also determined by the situation in which the person finds itself, and by the amount of conscious control the ego has over the personality.

I have often heard my clients say, *"Oh, but at home, I am very different than I am at work."* What that means is that they use their personality differently in different situations, not that they have different personalities. In every situation, three factors are driving your behavior: the decisions your *ego* makes based on your *personality* type and the *situation* you are in.

The following formulas clarify this:

Personality = Nature x Nurture

Behavior = Ego x Personality x Situation

Although this is somewhat simplified, it does help to understand several important things about the personality. Behaviors are situational fortunately, and although influenced by the personality, it does not necessarily dictate them.

This concludes our chapter on Jungian Typology 101, the fundamentals of Jung's type theory. In the next chapters, we will build on it to understand the dynamics of the personality.

Chapter 7

The Inferior Function: A Blessing in Disguise

When there is a light in the darkness which comprehends the darkness, darkness no longer prevails.

~ C.G. Jung, CW 14, § 345

The Inferior function is the fourth function of preference, and its key characteristic is that it is unconscious. It is there, always, and you basically have a limited or zero control over it. Instead, it has control over you. Jung called it inferior because it is the least developed, awkward, and slow. It is the capacity in yourself and others that you are the most frustrated with and distrustful of. It is the Achilles Heel of the personality, the "blind spot," the place of the Shakespearean "fatal flaw." It trips you up, makes you stumble, and fall. And the worst thing is that you cannot develop it. Instead, it develops you. It even comes to your aid in a time of great need. It is the function that is directly connected with the unconscious, which is where one's personal growth and transformation originate from. That is the good news.

Marie-Louise Von Franz, Jung's lifelong collaborator, describes the Inferior function as follows:

It is generally slow... Jung calls it infantile and tyrannical... The reaction of the superior function comes out quickly and well adapted, while many people have no idea where their Inferior function really is. For instance, Thinking types have no idea whether they have Feeling or what kind of Feeling it is. They have to sit half an hour and meditate as to whether they have Feelings about something and, if so, what they are... But it cannot be sped up. It does not help to get impatient. And naturally that is what is so discouraging about getting up the Inferior function: one has not the time for it.
(Von Franz, 1998, Chapter 1: General Characterization of the Inferior Function)

When people start analyzing their personalities, it usually becomes clear fairly quickly what their dominant function pair or temperament is. But then the question is which one of the two functions that make up a temperament is the dominant one? If for example, your dominant temperament is a combination of Sensation (S) and Thinking (T), you might find it hard to determine which one of the two is your dominant function.

The Inferior function can assist in identifying which one it is. Your type preference is determined as much by what you like and trust as by what you dislike and distrust. So, if you can discern your Inferior function, its opposite pole is the dominant function. You can discover your Inferior function by asking yourself which function you prefer the least, especially under stress. Or as Von Franz put it:

Practically, it is most helpful when one wants to find out their type to ask, what is the greatest cross for the person? Where is his greatest suffering? Where does he feel that he always knocks his head against the obstacle and suffers hell? That generally points to the Inferior function.
(Von Franz, 1998, Chapter 1: General Characterization of the Inferior Function)

My own experience with the Inferior function is that it feels like plodding through mud and snow on a winter's day. It can be painful, even akin to punishment. I cannot use it for a long time without going nuts. And if I compare myself to others for whom this function is dominant, I can feel terribly inadequate as well as completely fascinated. How do they do it, I wonder?

My Inferior function is Green Sensation, and I admire people with practical professions like accountants, mechanics, or carpenters. For me what they do is just magical. I once replaced the spark plugs on my car. It took me a while to figure it out, but once I had done it and the car started, it felt as if I had performed a miracle.

When confronted with our Inferior function we typically become agitated and experience strong emotions. The word "emotion" comes from the Latin *"emovere,"* meaning, "to move out, agitate." On the negative side, we can experience a strong distrust of and frustration with our Inferior function. On the positive side, we can experience a joy bordering on ecstasy when we accomplish something using our Inferior function. We can experience it both as a drain as well as a boost of energy.

There are four ways of dealing with our Inferior function:
- Fake it (which only works superficially)
- Work around it (which yields limited success)
- Deal with it and bite the bullet (which is painful)
- Work with it when it surfaces from the unconscious (win-win)

Most people develop some simple routines in their Inferior function, which help them "fake it" or "cover-up." These cover-ups are usually borrowed from others. The Yellow Intuitive type will develop some general practical routines, but nothing specific to a situation and nothing terribly efficient. The Green Sensation type will embrace an existing and accepted idea and call it an "innovation." The Red Feeling type will read a book and reproduce the thoughts in that book without really understanding them or thinking them through. The Blue Thinking type will imitate friendly gestures or expressions they pick up from others, like serving a drink, or sending some flowers or asking how someone is doing. Yet a Red Feeling type will quickly see that as disingenuous, or not "from the heart." People with strongly developed functions in the same area(s) as someone else's Inferior function will not be deceived, and will likely see through the inauthenticity of this behavior. As Von Franz put it:

You can always observe these "covering up" reactions by the fact that they are impersonal and banal and very collective. They have no convincing personal quality about them.
(Von Franz, 1998, Chapter 1: General Characterization of the Inferior Function)

I can illustrate these options with examples from my personal life. Faking it is not that hard. Most people do it. When it is time for me to prepare my tax return, my accountant asks me for a lot of information. Gathering this information severely taxes my limited capacity for Green Sensation. It takes me a long time, and when he asks about it, my standard answer is, "I'm working on it. I should have it for you shortly." This can go on for several days or even weeks. I give the impression that I'm really busy with it when in reality what I am doing is very limited.

I have also learned to work around it. In a society where Green Sensation is highly valued, like Dutch society, my lack in this area could be challenging. At school, for example, I did very well, aided by a well-developed Blue Thinking process and my dominant Yellow Intuition. It was still hard to perform the tasks associated with my Green Sensation function, but it was good for my development, as I had to work my way around it using my other functions.

A good example of biting the bullet is when I move to a different home. In the old home, I have practical routines that I cannot do without, that I am very dependent on. They are also unconscious, i.e., I do not realize how important they are until I cannot perform them any longer. For instance, one of the qualities of Green Sensation is to have a place for everything and everything in its place. That physical order of my living environment goes out the door when I move. As a result, it takes a deliberate, conscious effort to find my way again in a new environment. Where will I leave my keys? Where will I go to exercise? How do I cook food in this kitchen? Where can I go shopping in this neighborhood? Where is everything? The Green Sensation type will adapt to this new reality in days. For me it is a slow process, a real struggle that can even take weeks, if not months.

We can also work with it as it surfaces. For example, a new hard drive for my computer has been lying around for several months, but I have not felt like installing it. The other day I felt inspired, so I replaced the drive. The moment of inspiration was my window of opportunity. If I had not done it then, I would have had to wait for the next cycle of inspiration to come around which probably would have taken several months.

You Cannot Develop It; It Develops You!

Because the Inferior function is unconscious, you cannot develop it. Or, as Von Franz (1998, Chapter 1) put it when she drew an analogy to fishing, *"the fish will be too big for the rod."* In a sense, that is also the great beauty of it. This is the area in life we cannot control. It is a mystery, a big black box, and a source of great frustration. It is also the missing key we need to shape our destiny. It is said that this is the area in our life where the ego has to succumb to a higher power, the divine if you like, which then can intervene and allow miracles to happen. In the teams and individuals, I worked with; I witnessed the slow and thoughtful assimilation of the Inferior function leading to unexpected, mind-boggling results and to remarkable human transformations. The Inferior function always introduces new ways of looking at things and new ways of solving problems.

Usually, the Ego stands in the way of this process. It does not allow the Inferior function to be assimilated until a real crisis hits or a painstaking conscious choice is made to go with it. If I am in a very challenging situation, it is always my Green Sensation function that gets me through. Having tried to solve the problem with my Yellow Intuition, Blue Thinking, and Red Feeling, only Green Sensation is left to find a solution, and it does. For me, this often involves doing research, finding relevant information, cleaning up, and ordering my life. For the Green Sensation type, the solution is quite the opposite. That person needs to take a new idea seriously that it had previously discarded as nonsensical, work on it and see what it has to say (without being limited by the practical implications).

In her *Lectures on Jung's Typology,* Von Franz says:

> *It [the Inferior function] represents the despised part of the personality, the ridiculous and unadapted part, but also the part that builds up the connection with the unconscious and therefore holds the secret key to the unconscious totality of the person.*
> (Von Franz, 1998, Chapter 1: General Characterization of the Inferior Function)

My business partner and I once enlisted a consultant to help us organize and plan our business. This consultant had a strong Blue Thinking and Green Sensation preference, forming the Teal Technician Temperament, which was why we hired him. We were to define key weekly activities. It took us a long time to come up with these, and when we each had about four or five, he asked us to plot them in our agenda. At one point while doing this, I glanced at our consultant. I'll never forget the pity I saw on his face; he simply could not understand how difficult this was for us.

It worked the other way around too. Whenever we had a great idea about how our business could impact the lives and well-being of our clients' employees he would look at us and say, "I have to see it to believe it." We, in turn, could not understand how he could not see it. In the end, it was our success as a business that earned his respect. We had revenue and profits, which was the language he understood.

Another typical source of frustration for Yellow Intuition is the yearly tax return. It takes weeks for Yellow Intuition to complete whereas Green Sensation does it in days. My father is a Green Sensation type and very good at tax returns, so good in fact that whenever he recruits the help of an accountant or tax attorney he ends up correcting their work. He tried to help me with my tax returns, but could not understand why it took me so long.

Most Green Sensation types like opening mail because it contains new and interesting information they will want to process. But for my Yellow Intuition, the daily mail is yesterday's news and not interesting at all. This was a source of irritation and incomprehension between my father and me. Such a "sore spot" is indicative of the Inferior function.

The Inferior Function and the Shadow

The Inferior function as the unconscious function of the personality is where the Shadow resides. It is, for example, the area of the personality where you can be most easily attacked or persuaded, even brainwashed. For example, a Yellow Intuitive type can quite vividly see the potential and future of something, or the deeper underlying meaning and causes of a problem. At the same time, this type is not particularly adept in the practical, task-oriented skills that the Green Sensation exhibits so effortlessly. In a conflict, the Yellow Intuitive type can easily be discredited as "a dreamer who cannot get the job done," which is true, but it is only half the equation.

The opposite is also true. Let us say a Green Sensation CEO is leading a company, which means that for this CEO the devil is not in the details, but in the lack of vision. This CEO can excel in creating an efficient organization. At the same time, this CEO can easily be discredited by saying he or she "lacks the vision to lead this company and has to be replaced."

A Red Feeling child can struggle at school, especially in subjects like mathematics and physics. A Blue Thinking teacher might say to the parents, "Your child is not university material." This is of course not true because what the teacher fails to recognize is that that student's qualities are in relating to and understanding others, seeing human needs and having a sense of ethics and beauty. Such a child could very well be "university material" but then in the field of humanities.

In terms of brainwashing, there is the following problem. The child can be very easily persuaded by the teacher's logical Blue Thinking arguments. The child knows she or he cannot do the work alone, so the child "borrows" the teacher's logic and can ultimately adopt beliefs such as, "The imagination is unreliable, false and treacherous." This is how a teacher unaware of type can blindly impose their worldview on a child. What the Red Feeling child needs most is to be allowed to examine and think on his or her own, no matter how awkward or slow a process this may be.

Because it has control over you, the Inferior function can be both powerful and dangerous. When Von Franz gave her lectures on Jungian Typology in 1971, she was asked about the relationship between propaganda and the Inferior function. In her answer, she gave the example of Hitler in 1930 Germany. It is worthwhile to reproduce her full response here because it is such powerful evidence of the effect propaganda can have through the Inferior function:

Question: *Would you say that propaganda is mainly a field for the Inferior function?*

Von Franz: *Yes… Someone practicing such a low type of propaganda would know that it is not by reasonable talk that one gets the masses but by arousing emotion.*

Emotion can be aroused in everyone at the same time if you bring up the Inferior function, because as I said before, that is the emotional function. Therefore, if you speak to intellectuals you must arouse primitive Feelings! If you speak to university professors, you must not use scientific language because in that field their minds are clear and they will see through all the snares in your speech. If you want to get a lie across, you must substantiate your lie with a lot of Feeling and emotion. Since university professors will on the average have inferior Feeling, they will fall for that at once.

Hitler had the art of doing this… At times, Hitler would at first be quite uncertain. He would try out his themes like a pianist, mentioning a little of this and a little of that. He would be pale and nervous, and his SS men would get all worked up because the Führer did not seem to be in form. But he was just trying out the ground.

Then he would notice that if he brought up a particular subject, it would arouse emotion, so then he would just go full tilt for that! That's the demagogue. When he feels that inferior side, he knows where the complexes are, and that is what he goes for.

One must argue in a primitive, emotional way, the way in which the Inferior function would argue. Hitler did not think that out. It was the fact that he was caught in his own inferiority, which gave him that talent.

(Von Franz, 1998, Chapter 4: The Role of the Inferior Function in Psychic Development)

It is said that after the war when German civilians were confronted with the horrors of concentration camps, they would say: "Wir haben es nicht gewusst." Which means "We did not know." Psychologically that is probably true since they were caught up in their inferior function. And Hitler was not the first nor will he be the last political leader to exploit this. Or the last person for that matter, because it happens every day, only on a much smaller scale. Cults are a good example of this mechanism. But it is also used in a more honorable profession like Marketing to create a dependency on a product.

There is a solution that is simple but not easy. If we do not want to be subject to unconscious manipulation, awareness of our fourth preference is at least as important as awareness of our first. That is a meaningful form of freedom. It is what John Beebe, Jungian analyst and author of *Energies and Patterns in Psychological Type,* calls the *backbone* of the personality:

> *When there is development of both the superior and the inferior functions, we can speak of a 'spine' of consciousness that gives a personality backbone.*
> (Beebe, 2017, Ch. 8)

Developing a strong backbone is the way to use the Inferior function positively, in a way that is positive, moral and ethical. There is just as much positive as negative potential in the shadow. Perhaps even more positive potential. For the purpose of creating a "spine of consciousness" I have put together a limited overview of these positive and negative potentials and how they can be used depending on your type.

The Positive and Negative Shadow of the Inferior Function

The Inferior function can be our fatal flaw as well as our savior and vehicle for growth and transformation. Awareness of this dynamic provides a significant advantage. The negative Shadow is something you want to circumvent carefully to ensure it does not trip you up. The positive Shadow is something you want to embrace and integrate every chance you get. Below is an overview of the positive and negative characteristics of the four functions of consciousness when they are the Inferior function.

Dominant Intuition with Inferior Sensation

Dominant Intuition	Perceives the potential development of something, that which is not yet visible, whether it is in the outer world or the inner world. Focuses on the big picture and can see in a split second all kinds of interesting and relevant interconnections and opportunities.
Negative Sensation	Does not see the physical, tangible reality, even if it is right in front of them. Can neglect the physical body, its warning messages (like hunger) and its needs (like sleep). Is not aware of time passing and cannot plan in detail. An object is described in vague terms like that "thing" or "stuff." Does not like any type of information processing whether it is taxes, e-mail or filling in forms. Often lacks discipline and can have addictions to a negative Sensation activity like binge eating.
Positive Sensation (Redeeming Shadow)	Will research and find relevant information on a subject that is important. Is unconsciously drawn to certain physical activities like yoga, athletics, sex, or cooking because of their symbolic and transformational qualities. It is not by choice, it happens from the unconscious, and it brings new life to the dominant function: Intuition.

Dominant Sensation with Inferior Intuition

Dominant Sensation	Perceives concrete, tangible reality in the here and now. Remembers facts in a differentiated, detailed way. Processes factual and practical information with great ease.
Negative Intuition	Has negative and dark suspicions of something unknown, disastrous premonitions of impending doom and gloom. Sees danger lurking behind every corner. The future either does not exist, or it exists as something ominous. Change is something intangible, unsettling, and will be met with pessimism. Stuck, in the here and now, believing life will always be the same or at least should be. Can have an unusual partiality for mystery novels or horror stories.
Positive Intuition (Redeeming Shadow)	Will have flashes of Intuition and great insight, which are often mind-boggling and difficult to process, like a sudden understanding of the meaning of life. Is unconsciously drawn to and fascinated by things that point to the supernatural and metaphysical, like mystical texts or religious objects. It is not by choice, it happens from the unconscious, and it brings new life to the dominant function: Sensation.

Dominant Thinking with Inferior Feeling

Dominant Thinking	Creates a logical order by analyzing information and structuring it. Likes to know what something is and what can be achieved with it. Can be critical and challenging with the purpose of understanding or testing someone's knowledge.
Negative Feeling	Feeling can be naïve and childlike, like a dog wagging its tail. Warmth and deep affection for spouse and children, but he or she neither knows nor feels it. Holds strong but naïve values and loyalties edging on fanaticism. Very black and white value judgments: I like you, or I don't. Not a good judge of people due to positive or negative prejudices, which can lead to the wrong choice of partners. Can exhibit an uninhibited display of affection and feel like a victim when rejected.
Positive Feeling (Redeeming Shadow)	Will suddenly realize that care, compassion, and love for one's neighbor are important values and feels a deep appreciation for people. Is unconsciously drawn to certain friends or family members for whom a genuine and warm affection is felt. The affection can be misplaced or misdirected, but it is only by voicing it that this is discovered. For whom or what affection is felt is not a choice: it happens from the unconscious, and conscious engagement brings new life to the dominant function: Thinking.

Dominant Feeling with Inferior Thinking

Dominant Feeling	Good judge of people and easy to make friends with. Compassionate and self-sacrificing by nature. Strong sense of ethical values that affect the human condition in a positive way.
Negative Thinking	Limited thoughts that are adhered to like dogmas or absolute truths. When challenged will more fanatically adhere to dogma. Can be cold, use people for personal gain, and abandon a relationship when no longer useful.
Positive Thinking (Redeeming Shadow)	Simple, clear, and understandable thought processes. Pure and elementary logic, like 2+2=4. Further logical constructs develop from there. Thinks things through and weighs the pros and cons. Assumptions are investigated through logical analysis. Can feel a strong attraction to certain schools of thought, science or philosophy. This does not happen by choice, it happens from the unconscious, and conscious engagement with it brings new life to the dominant function: Feeling.

This concludes the chapter on the Inferior function, the area of the personality where a person is the most frustrated and distrustful. It is also the area where one feels the strongest emotions, be they negative emotions or pure ecstasy. And yet it is the most critical element for our personal growth and ultimately transformation.

It is not just on a personal level that we have an Inferior function. Different cultures have this as well. Let us look at our own Western culture as an example next.

CHAPTER 8

THINKING AND FEELING: THE GREAT DIVIDE

It was the deeper, more durable question of where human beings find soul when a mechanistic view of the universe dominates the collective imagination.

~ Mark Vernon, Philosophy and Life Blog, 2011

Western civilization is characterized by the dominance of the Blue Thinking function, which began to surface and develop at the end of the Middle Ages. It has transformed Western society and has been both a blessing and a curse, as we shall see in the brief history of this function in Western culture next.

Brief History of the Blue Thinking Function in Western Culture

In the Middle Ages, European society was dominated by the church, a divinely ordained monarchy and the aristocracy who owned most of the natural resources and subjected the ordinary people to taxation and serfdom. In this class-based society, people remained in the class into which they born into for their entire lives. It was not until the 16th and 17th centuries that the Age of Enlightenment brought about a revolution in philosophy, art, science, religion, and politics.

The philosopher and mathematician René Descartes laid the foundation for 17th-century rationalism with the statement, "*Cogito ergo sum*", or "*I think, therefore I am.*" Groundbreaking discoveries by the astronomers Copernicus and Galileo revealed that not the Earth but the sun was the center of the solar system, much to the dismay of the pope who had the matter investigated by the Roman Inquisition. In 1633, Galileo was found guilty of heresy, forced to recant under the threat of torture and placed under house arrest for the remainder of his life.

Half a century later the mathematician, astronomer, and physicist Isaac Newton developed the concepts of the laws of gravity and motion, which form the foundations of modern astronomy and physics. This resulted in Galileo's formal pardoning by the pope on behalf of the Catholic Church, but not until 1992. The "enlightened" Thinking function of philosophers like Thomas Hobbes, Hugo Grotius, and John Locke developed the concepts of autonomy of individuals and the right to property. This was unheard of at the time because the church, monarchy, and aristocracy owned most property.

In 1568, the Dutch became the first Europeans to revolt against this medieval structuring of society. When the Duke of Alba led the

Spanish Inquisition in the Netherlands and raised taxes, the Dutch soon had enough. Led by William of Orange, they fought the Eighty Years' War of Independence against Philip II of Spain, sovereign of the great Habsburg monarchy. The Republic of the Seven United Provinces of the Netherlands was born. This Dutch victory challenged the concept of the divine ordination of kings, and across Europe people gradually realized that monarchies could be challenged and overthrown.

After this victory for the Dutch, the feudal structure of medieval society continued to disintegrate. A big turning point was the American War of Independence (1775-1783), which resulted in the thirteen North American colonies of Great Britain declaring independence and forming the United States of America. Not much later, in 1789, the French Revolution broke out, ending 800 years of monarchy in France, and forging the French Republic. Out of the French Republic came the French Empire with Napoleon as its first emperor. He broke with the medieval custom of divine ordination and coronation by the Church. Instead, he simply crowned himself! This action was typical of an independent thinker such as Napoleon. The separation of church and state now became an accepted principle in Western culture.

These major changes were catalysts for the Blue Thinking achievements that followed: The Industrial Revolution and Capitalism. Technological innovations such as the steam engine, chemicals, and machinery transformed an agricultural society into an industrial one. Cities expanded rapidly, roads, canals, and railroad tracks were used for transportation, and factories replaced farms as centers of economic production and employment.

Money was introduced as a means of exchange, and economics was developed as a discipline by the Scottish philosopher Adam Smith, who was the first to postulate the principles of a capitalist economy.

After Europe, the United States took the lead in technological innovation with the invention of the automobile, the airplane, the personal computer, data processing and the establishment of the Apollo program that put a man on the moon. Today, we have powerful technologies like smartphones, the Internet, and social media that connect people globally.

These achievements are phenomenal and the result of a highly developed Blue Thinking function supported by both Yellow Intuition and Green Sensation. The two dominant temperaments of the Blue Thinking function are the NT Temperament, the Inventor; and the ST Temperament, the Technician. What we have witnessed in the past 500 years is how the Technician Temperament builds what the Inventor Temperament designs. The enormous impact of these powerful forces working in tandem has defined Western civilization and made it into what it is today, for better or for worse.

The word "achievement" itself is a word that is typical for the Blue Thinking function. We talk, for instance, about scientific or technological achievement. Achievement in this sense should not be confused with progress. Progress is a more generic term that can apply to each function. For Intuition, progress means accepting new and radical ideas, for Feeling it is creating connection and harmony, for Sensation, it is establishing a practical order.

Needless to say, these achievements have also cast a shadow. Only a society that is so proficient at Thinking could have developed the military technology that Western culture has today. Employing this military capacity is also typical of the Extraverted Thinking function in its drive for power and control over its environment.

The military power we have now is enough to destroy civilization as we know it, and the Blue Thinking function can be ruthless when it comes to the human condition. European nations exploited colonies in Asia and Africa for hundreds of years. Here, in America, European colonists decimated the Native American Indian population. Africans were kidnapped and imported to work as slaves. Then consider wars. The military technology that was so cleverly fabricated by the Blue Thinking function was able to kill untold millions of people in two World Wars.

The area where these achievements have cast an equally long shadow is on the opposite end of the spectrum: the Red Feeling function, which pays an enormous price. The psychological law is that the more advanced the progress on one end of the spectrum, the higher the price is that has to be paid at the other end of the spectrum for a system to maintain its balance. It is safe to say that in Western civilization this imbalance has reached a critical stage. This raises the question how the Red Feeling function could act as a countervailing force?

The Red Feeling Function as a Countervailing Force

The Red Feeling function is the function of consciousness that evaluates the human condition, and the fundamental issues of human existence, such as physical health, mental health, financial health, relationships, education, conflict, personal growth, art, and the health of the planet's natural environment. The Red Feeling cannot bear to hurt, let alone kill another human being.
There *have* been counter movements in Western society, intended to balance the Blue Thinking in society with Red Feeling.

Examples of this in the 20th century are the suffragette movement for women's voting rights, the American Civil Rights Movement, unions, equal rights for women, equal rights for LGBT people, the Flower Power movement of the 1960s, and the return to organically farmed foods, just to name a few. The Beatles scored a hit with *All You Need is Love*, and John Lennon protested the Vietnam War with *Give Peace a Chance*. Has it worked? Are the changes in society real and heartfelt? Has the landscape changed?

A limited statistical review can provide us with some constructive feedback on the state of the human condition and the price it has paid for 150 years of Industrial Revolution:
- One in five American adults suffers from mental illness (depression, mental disorders)
- One in 25 American adults suffer from serious mental illness that is debilitating
- Healthcare spending per person in 2010 was 50 (!) times what it was in 1960, but the impact on life expectancy is relatively low (47 years in 1900, 71 years in 1960, 77 years in 2010. In other words, spending 50 times as much has led to an increase of six years)
- Prescription of opioid pain relievers has skyrocketed in the last 25 years, leading to 20,000 overdose deaths in 2016
- Industrial waste products have polluted our natural environment: massive garbage patches of plastic pollution in the oceans can be seen from space, one of which is twice the size of Texas
- Since 1800 we have emitted 2,000 gigatons of carbon dioxide (from coal, oil, and gas) increasing the concentration in the atmosphere by 40% more than its highest rate in the last 400,000 years
- Two World Wars fought with modern technology have resulted in 68 million casualties

In short, the achievements of the Blue Thinking function have come at a considerable price. And if we look at our education systems, the imbalance continues there. Western education is oriented towards the Blue Thinking function and emphasizes cognitive skills that are used to think, read, learn, remember, reason, and solve problems. The future of the economy is supposed to lie in STEM Education: Science, Technology, Engineering, and Mathematics. A description of cognitive skills on www.reference.com is, coincidentally, a good definition of the Blue Thinking function:

Logic abilities enable mature thought processes, including analysis and deductive reasoning. Developing logic allows an individual to think in abstract terms and reach conclusions and solutions by using existing knowledge to evaluate new information. Advanced thought and reasoning also help individuals ask questions, experiment with trial and error and express creativity.
(Fiddis, 2017)

But what happens to children with a dominant Red Feeling function? For them, education must be incredibly uninteresting and challenging, and they suffer self-esteem issues because their specific abilities are typically undervalued. The frustration of the Feeling function with Western education is well expressed by the English author and graphic novelist, Neil Gaiman:

I've been making a list of the things they don't teach you at school. They don't teach you how to love somebody. They don't teach you how to be famous. They don't teach you how to be rich or how to be poor. They don't teach you how to walk away from someone you don't love any longer. They don't teach you how to know what's going on in someone else's mind. They don't teach you what to say to someone who's dying. They don't teach you anything worth knowing.
(Gaiman, 2011)

The Red Feeling Function as a Source of Renewal and Growth

If it is true that the Red Feeling Function is the inferior function in the Western world, then that is where our renewal, growth, and regeneration will come from. As Marie-Louise von Franz, Carl Jung's faithful collaborator wrote:

In the realm of the inferior function there is a great concentration of life, so that as soon as the superior function is worn out—begins to rattle and lose

oil like an old car—if people succeed in turning to their inferior function, they will rediscover a new potential of life.
(Von Franz, 1998, Chapter 1: General Characterization of the Inferior Function)

In the life of an individual, organization or nation, the superior function will sooner or later start showing serious shortcomings. Life has become too lopsided, too out of balance. After standing on one leg for too long, we need to switch to the other leg. But what if we are unaware of our "other leg"? Or, if we are aware of it, but despise, shame, and ridicule it? The Red Feeling function is sometimes mockingly identified as "Holding hands and singing 'Kumbaya.'" If we stubbornly keep standing on one and the same leg, we will fall over. And not only will we fall over: we will have lost an opportunity for growth, development, and reaching our potential.

The Blue Thinking function loves to discuss and argue a point, to have control and power and win arguments. But taken to the extreme, this means nothing gets done; there is only opposition and conflict, a show of power, the clashing of armor. The important question to answer is: How can we use our Red Feeling function to Think better? And how can we use our Blue Thinking function to Feel better? The purpose of polarities is to complement rather than conflict with each other.

We can use team sports as an example here. A Blue Thinking approach to building a winning team is to buy the best players you can, hire the best coach, provide the team with excellent facilities, and sit back and watch the team win championships. I have seen this strategy attempted often but never seen it succeed. It is always the best *team* that wins the championship, not the best collection of individuals.

This might come as a surprise, but teamwork is actually a "specialty" of the Red Feeling function. It can make some outstanding contributions to good teamwork, like:

- Understanding what motivates and drives people.
- Sharing the power of unity and harmony.
- Making use of the unique contribution someone can make.
- Being aware of the human impact of decisions.
- Embracing human dialogue and creativity in problem-solving.
- Handling stress and adapting to change.

Emotional Intelligence as the Next Evolutionary Step for Western Culture

Perhaps the greatest contribution to the recovery of the Red Feeling function in business comes from psychologist and author Daniel Goleman and many others with the concept of "Emotional Intelligence" or "Emotional Quotient" (EQ), which was introduced in 1995. It is a model that expresses how we connect to our own Feelings and to those of others. Most interpretations of the model contain the following elements:

Self-Awareness   Know your Feeling values and why you have them. Do they reflect true needs or false needs? This provides a basis for sound decision-making as well as a moral compass.

Self-Regulation   Handle stressful emotions in effective ways, so they do not cripple you or interfere with your goals. Tuning into these emotions so that you may learn from them (because every emotion has a function).

Motivation   Know what you are passionate about and be able to connect that passion with what you are pursuing personally and

	professionally.
Empathy	Resonate with what someone is experiencing emotionally as well as understand and respect their Feeling values. Show that you care.
Social Skills	Connect with others and build healthy, lasting and collaborative relationships.

Research at the Harvard Business School indicates that EQ is twice as important as IQ and technical skills combined in determining who will be successful in their careers and personal lives. This is a surprising discovery to those of us who always thought that IQ was the dominant predictor of job success. But as Manfred Kets de Vries, a professor at the French INSEAD business school, and renowned coach of executive leaders says: *"A gram of feelings is worth more than a ton of facts."* For example, if, as a leader, you can show that you genuinely care, people will be much more motivated to follow you.

In the current economic work environment, IQ and technical skills are *threshold competencies*, i.e., they are a basic requirement people need to meet when they enter the workforce. After that EQ becomes the most important differentiator.

In education, there are now SEL (Social and Emotional Learning) programs that help children to learn SEL skills, which are equivalent to the Emotional Intelligence skills described above. A recent study by Roger Weissberg of the University of Illinois at Chicago showed that 38% of the children in SEL programs improved their Grade Point Average (GPA), misbehavior dropped by 28%, suspensions fell by 44%, and attendance rose. This is huge and at the same time it should not come as a surprise because learning at schools is a social process. These results demonstrate that there is great power in things like empathy, care, connection and respectfully disagreeing with each other at schools. SEL boosts social competence and mental health of students as well as the climate at a school. It even reduces drug use.

It is not a question of *either* STEM *or* SEL but *both* STEM *and* SEL education in schools in order harness the power of polarities. The Blue Thinking types will naturally be attracted to STEM and the Red Feeling types to SEL programs. When combined, both feel at home, successful and appreciated within the same school. But not only that, SEL and STEM education *will strengthen each other*. Research by Roger Weissberg has shown that at schools where SEL is implemented academic performance improves significantly:

> *Compared to controls, SEL participants demonstrated significantly improved social and emotional skills, attitudes, behavior, and academic performance that reflected an 11-percentile-point gain in achievement.*
> (Weissberg, 2011, p. 1)

The discoveries made by the Emotional Intelligence movement, show that the Red Feeling function can actually help us to think better and reach our full potential. The main challenge is to transcend dualistic "either-or" consciousness and understand how the recovery of the Red Feeling function in Western culture will ignite the entire personality and the whole culture, not just a part of it.

CHAPTER 9

FALSIFICATION OF TYPE: THE PROBLEM OF THE GREAT PRETENDER

As a rule, whenever such a falsification of type takes place as a result of parental influence, the individual becomes neurotic later, and can be cured only by developing the attitude consonant with his nature.

~ C.G. Jung, CW 6, § 560

We are most alive, at home, happy, confident, and competent when we follow the natural preferences of our personality, our so-called true type. It provides us with a healing and uplifting experience and has a positive impact on our self-esteem because we are using our unique capabilities. I often tell my clients "Yes, you do need to develop your weaknesses so that they don't trip you up, but your value to an employer lies in how you use your dominant function. That's the function of your personality you will be rewarded for the most to use."

Falsification of type, on the other hand, drains our life energy. It occurs when we decide to develop and rely on another function and attitude in the personality than our innate one. An individual can feel exhausted, unproductive at work or have difficulty learning a new skill. Physical symptoms include headaches and a weak immune system leading to illnesses. Emotionally, there can be lack of self-confidence and joy, leading to depression.

Falsification of type usually occurs in the process of creating an idealized self-image so as to be accepted by others. But pretending to be someone you are not has an inner price, and eventually the journey of "becoming who you were before you became who you are" has to begin. Most of us suffer from this to some extent, and the origins can be traced biographically to our family of origin and the culture we live in. Functions other than our natural preferences are acknowledged, stimulated, approved, and cultivated, while our natural preferences are met with discouragement, negative judgment, and rejection.

There are many examples of the dynamic that can lead to a falsification of type. For example, an extraverted and Red Feeling mother will say to an introverted Blue Thinking child, "Stop spending so much time in your room, go outside and make some friends." For her, it is incomprehensible that her child has only one friend. "And what do they do?", she exclaims, "They play chess!". She used to have a bunch of friends when she was young, and they would go out and do fun things, and she cannot understand what is "wrong" with her son.

Or the Introverted Blue Thinking father might say to his extraverted Red Feeling child, "You're not going to the mall with your friends this weekend until you've done all your math assignments. Without math, you have no future." Or the extraverted Green Sensation father will tell the Yellow Intuitive child, "When I was your age I played sports from dawn to dusk, and when I came home I did my chores. You just sit here and daydream. Your life is wasting away.

You're going to make yourself useful around here. And I'm going to sign you up for basketball, and volunteer as the coach. That will teach you."

Marie-Louise von Franz gives an example of a boy with a Red Feeling function whose family have a preference for Blue Thinking:

Suppose a boy is born a Feeling type in an intellectually ambitious family. His surroundings will exert pressure upon him to become an intellectual, and his original predisposition as a Feeling type will be thwarted or despised. Usually, in such a case, he is unable to become a Thinking type: that would be one step too far. But he might well develop Sensation or Intuition, one of the auxiliary functions, so as to be relatively better adapted to his surroundings; his main function is simply 'out' in the milieu in which he grows up.
(Von Franz, 1998, Chapter 1: General Characterization of the Inferior Function)

In short, falsification of type occurs when a child develops a coping mechanism that uses more unnatural personality preferences to please its family, be accepted, and have a place. But when this idealized self takes root, and the much yearned for acceptance and place in the family are achieved, what then? The child is stuck, afraid to let go of this false type because of the enormous investment. The cost of changing back is too high: the child is afraid to face the loss of acceptance, the pain of being rejected and wounded again. The more unconscious we are of this, the more compulsively we adhere to this idealized self-image. If this anxiety driven compulsion does not become conscious, a common neurosis that can develop is an obsessive compulsive disorder, for example, around cleanliness (fear of contamination), or religion (fear of hell), or illness and aging (fear of death).

One way to break out of this is to ask others for feedback. Others can see the "Great Pretender" in you much more easily than you can. But ask them to be gentle, as it can be a painful realization. As parents, there is much we can do to prevent this from happening, but only if we are aware and mindful of our own and the child's type. It is OK to push him or her to develop in certain areas in which they are "clumsy" or find "difficult," but not to the extreme, and not by withholding love, approval, and affection.

In the course of your life, your parents' types and/or the culture you live in may result in developing a personality preference that is not your own, and you become stressed as a result. Children are very adaptable, but sooner or later life forces a return to the natural preference, the true type. This can happen through burnout, illness, a failed career, or some other breakdown. For a return to a healthy state of being a recovery needs to occur, a total reboot of one's life. Fortunately, the natural preferences are always there and once used will respond very quickly and come alive in the personality. As Von Franz once said, *"They are like fish that can now return happily to the water."* At that point, all the time spent developing functions that were not the natural preference pays off. The personality is more complete than it ever was before.

In my own typological development, I was clearly an extraverted Yellow Intuition type from early on. I always initiated new activities, always looked for some new experience or possibility to pursue. I would round up my friends to play soccer in the afternoon, or I would start electronics projects with them. At one point, I designed a "parent alarm system" at a friend's house. We built and placed a detector made from aluminum foil under the rug in the hallway outside his room, and if his mother came to check on him, a warning light next to his bed turned on, and he knew he had to hide his book, turn off his reading light, and pretend to be asleep.

I also loved reading fiction, and my Intuition was so strong that while reading a book I was transported to an entirely different world. In my mind's eye, I "saw" and experienced every "scene" in the book in great detail. There was no need for virtual reality; I was living inside my inner vision. Because I wanted to do well at school—and I knew it was also important to my parents that I did—

I developed my Blue Thinking function quite well. Together with my Yellow Intuition, I developed a solid Intuitive Thinking Temperament (NT), which fueled my academic success. But refining this function to the extent I did was more a matter of necessity and survival than of free choice.

My Red Feeling function, which really is my second function, was not so well matured. When I really wanted to do something, my father would often rationalize it away. He would say, "Is this really necessary? I don't see what good it will do." Or, he would resort to a much-used Dutch expression (a country with a history of moderation): "Just act normal, that's already crazy enough." It was not enough for him that I was passionate about what I wanted to do.

Later in life, in my 20s and 30s, I attended lots of self-development workshops where my Red Feeling function was welcome and where I could develop it. If you look around, a lot of these retreats and courses center on the Red Feeling function. This eventually led to a career change when I was 36: from an economist and management consultant to an entrepreneur with a focus on learning and team development. That was where I realized my true power as a professional, and I built up a successful business in the Netherlands.

I call falsification of type the "problem of the Great Pretender" for a reason. We are frequently unaware of what is happening. We have taken "fake it until you make it" to an extreme. We have identified with the function we are trying to emulate, and all our self-esteem is dependent on it and to anyone who asks we say: "This is who I really am!" If we continue with "And don't you dare doubt it!" we know we have touched the sensitive nerve of type falsification.

I also have witnessed the dire consequences of type falsification. A wonderful woman in a workshop I was teaching was a warm Red Feeling type and was desperately trying to be a Blue Thinking type in both her work and her marriage. I could see how unbelievably stressful this was for her and I told her she needed to be aware of this. About a year later, I met her employer and asked how her employee was doing. She told me that she had been hospitalized with a stroke. She was only 38 years old. I think her type falsification caused this, and to this day I regret not being able to help prevent this mishap. Jung warned of this in no uncertain terms:

> *A reversal of type often proves exceedingly harmful to the physiological well-being of the organism, usually causing acute exhaustion.*
> (Jung, CW 6, § 333)

When we use our natural preferences, we tend to experience ease, flow, curiosity, and excitement. We are also relatively good at it. If others compliment us, we may be taken aback and respond, "Really, you think that was good? I thought anyone could do that." No, when you find your "superpower," it is precisely that: something you can do better than anyone else. And you may be surprised or even disappointed when others are not able to do what you can.

I hope these examples illustrate how the power of polarities can work against an individual, a family, a team, or organization when the concept of opposite, mutually exclusive yet complementary forces is misunderstood. All roads lead to Rome, it is said. I would like to add that those roads are there for a reason, the same way all the different personality types are there for a reason.

Finally, I would like to mention what economists call an "opportunity cost" to type falsification. An "opportunity cost" is the loss of the potential benefit of an opportunity that differs from the one chosen. It is what you forego to get something. The opportunity cost of type falsification is the lack of development of the unique capabilities that lie nascent in your true type, the superpower that makes you different and valuable to others. It is the most important reason why I developed the model presented in this book, and I hope it will make finding your true type relatively quick and easy.

My experience teaching workshops has been that roughly 20% of my participants get their personality right the first time and 20% get it wrong. The other 60% is more or less accurate. This greatly depends on the degree of self-awareness. If people have experienced a degree of introspection and personality analysis, they almost always get it right. One way of looking at this is that in 20% of the cases there is a falsification of type and in 60% a degree of falsification. Their personality profile is still of value because it is something they can reflect on and receive feedback on from others. It starts the process of discovery of their true type.

For the purpose of discovering one's true type, I have created a free self-assessment that people can take as often as they want, reflect on the results, and find their true type in as few repeat efforts as possible. But it all starts with the assumption that the first result you get is not your true type. This, of course, is the opposite of what most personality instruments propagate. What they should tell you but don't is that that there is no such thing as a scientifically valid personality self-assessment, at least not in the sense of a thermometer or speedometer. Anyone with rudimentary knowledge of an assessment can fake it. And any self-assessment is not objective, but subjective by definition. That does not mean statistics and specifically psychometrics are not valuable. One can and should improve the quality of an assessment with psychometrics, but do not expect an exact and scientific measurement of the personality like you get on the speedometer of your car.

Marie-Louise von Franz took it a step further when she said:

The diagnosis of type is very difficult, for people are often in stages where they are sure they are of a certain type, but you need the whole case history

to know whether it is only a momentary stage of that person. For example, someone says that he is an extrovert, but that means nothing; you have carefully to take the whole biography of that person to make a relatively safe diagnosis. Up till now we have had no absolutely safe, scientific foundation for our theory and we do not pretend to have one.
(Von Franz, 1971, Chapter 3: The Four Rational Types)

Since Von Franz spoke these words at a lecture at the Jung Institute in Zürich, a considerable amount of research has been done indicating that the dimensions that Jung identified do indeed exist. At the same time, it takes careful self-evaluation to determine one's own type.

Personally, I do this by asking certain questions about their personality profile. It is a quick and effective way to build a bridge between the profile someone just received and their personal reality. Soon it becomes clear whether their profile reflects their true type or not. Below is a sample of questions I tend to ask:

1. What are practical examples of how you use your most dominant function?
2. What are practical examples of how you use your second function?
3. How effective is your use of these functions? What are you doing well and what are areas for development?
4. How could you improve your overall effectiveness?
5. What are practical examples of your aversion to your polar opposite?
6. In your own words, what is your most negative judgment of your polar opposite?
7. What positive impact could your polar opposite have on your effectiveness? How could it help you achieve your goals?
8. If you had to choose one thing to do differently from now on, what would that be?

I encourage you to get your personal profile online and do this exercise for yourself. You can do this by taking the personality indicator I developed. You can access it at: https://polaritylearning.com/form.html

There is one more thing concerning the "diagnosis of type"... I believe that within the next few decades we will find a way to measure someone's personality preferences objectively. This will not end falsification of type, but it will be much easier to identify one's true type accurately. I believe it will be done by analyzing certain autonomous functions of the body and/or using Artificial Intelligence (AI). I have seen glimpses of this: for example, using physical exercises to determine function and attitude preference. Action Type is a school of typology that says that your type determines the way your body deals with gravity. Another example is brain research. Quite a bit of research into brain activity has already been done, but without conclusive results.

Chapter 10

The Typological Octahedron

> *The four functions are somewhat like the four points of the compass; they are just as arbitrary and just as indispensable. Nothing prevents our shifting the cardinal points as many degrees as we like in one direction or the other, or giving them different names. It is merely a question of convention and intelligibility. But one thing I must confess: I would not for anything dispense with this compass on my psychological voyages of discovery.*
>
> ~ C.G. Jung, CW 6, § 958-9

Jung used the octahedron (or double pyramid) as a model for the psyche, which he fundamentally believed exists out of quaternities. I learned this from the Chicago Jungian analyst and author, Robert Moore who is known for his work on archetypes. After one of my visits, he gave me a small crystal shaped as an octahedron. He said Jung called it the "Diamond Body" and that it was an archetypal model of the psyche. Two decades later this gift proved to be of great value when I tried to decipher and model the structure and dynamics of the personality.

To my surprise, when I sat down one evening and started drawing, I found it a very suitable diagram to represent the personality because it is a geometrical form with which one can model three polarities (in our case T/F, S/N, and I/E). The result was this figure.

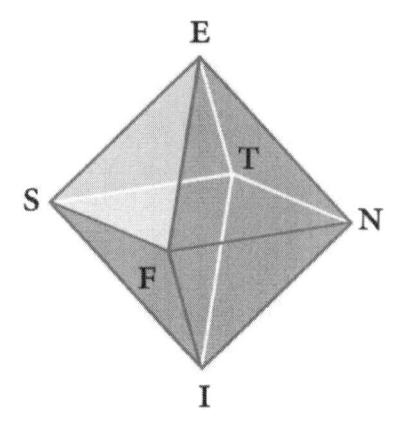

The octahedron is comprised of two opposing pyramids with the same base, which has four corners, one for each function: Thinking (T), Feeling (F), Sensation (S) and Intuition (N). It has eight triangular lateral faces that meet at the North and South pole of the double pyramid. The introverted apex (I) is located at the bottom, the extraverted apex (E) is located at the top.

The Base of the Octahedron

It is paramount that in determining someone's type, we first look at the horizontal plane or base of the pyramid. It consists of the four functions: Blue Thinking (T), Red Feeling (F), Green Sensation (S) and Yellow Intuition (N). In the diagram below the base of the pyramid is seen from the top.

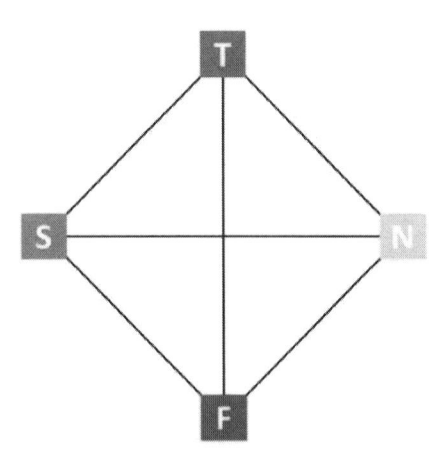

In *Psychological Types* Carl Jung describes how these functions do not work in isolation, but rather in *combinations* or *pairs*. Specifically, one of the perceiving function on the horizontal axis above (S or N) teams up with one judging function on the vertical axis above (T or F) to form a particular combination. He gives a brief description what these combinations look like:

> *The resulting combinations present the familiar picture of, for instance, practical Thinking allied with Sensation, speculative Thinking forging ahead with Intuition, artistic Intuition selecting and presenting its images with the help of Feeling-values, philosophical Intuition systematizing its vision into comprehensible thought by means of a powerful intellect, and so on.*
> (Jung, CW 6, § 669)

To clarify, what Jung is describing here are the following combinations of perceiving and judging functions:

ST – Sensation and Thinking	*"practical Thinking allied with Sensation"*
NT – Intuition and Thinking	*"speculative Thinking forging ahead with Intuition"*
NF – Intuition and Feeling	*"artistic Intuition selecting and presenting its images with the help of Feeling-values"*
NT – Intuition and Thinking	*"philosophical Intuition systematizing its vision into comprehensible thought by means of a powerful intellect"*

Interestingly enough, in this description, Jung leaves out the Sensation and Feeling (SF) pair and mentions the Intuition and Thinking (NT) pair twice. This is most likely the result of a "Jungian slip." Jung was someone with a strong preference for the NT pair and the opposite SF pair was the least familiar to him. He most likely left it out unconsciously. But if he had included a description of SF it might have been something along these lines: *"practical Feeling providing help in times of need."*

In summary, we have four fundamental pairs of perceiving and judging functions in the personality:
ST – Sensation and Thinking
SF – Sensation and Feeling
NT – Intuition and Thinking
NF – Intuition and Feeling

Next, we will see how these pairs form temperaments and what the meaning of these temperaments in our daily lives.

The Four Temperaments

The four Judging and Perceiving function pairs are the fundamental building blocks of the personality, and each represents a temperament: a deep underlying typological pattern from which people observe, process information and act. It shows up in patterns of (inter)action, talents, needs, values, and roles people play. The table below shows how the functions team up to produce four distinct temperaments: *Technician, Helper, Inventor* and *Visionary*.

		Perceiving	
		What is (S)	**What could be (N)**
Judging	**Logical impact (T)**	*ST - Technician:* Logical and matter-of-fact	*NT - Inventor:* Logical and ingenious
	Personal impact (F)	*SF - Helper:* Personal and caring	*NF - Visionary:* Personal and insightful

The table below gives an overview of all the different qualities that can be found in each of these four temperaments.

Temperament	ST	SF	NT	NF
Name	Technician	Helper	Inventor	Visionary
Drive	Productive self-discipline	Help people in real need.	Ingenious achievement and innovation.	Personal growth and self-determination
Need for	Clear structures and boundaries	To belong and contribute	Competence and insights	Meaning and inspiration
Interest	Practical knowledge	Practical relationships	Transformative knowledge	Transformative relationships
Contribution	Structure, build and maintain things	Care, nurture, support and keep people well	Discover and apply new knowledge	Create compelling narrative for change
Work ethic	Efficiency	Service	Effectiveness	Motivation
Work focus	Tactics, policies, and procedures	Practical support and teamwork	Strategy and long-term planning	Ideals, purpose, and values.
Types of Careers	Engineering, Law, Research, Computing, Mechanics, Accounting, Practical Science	Healthcare, Customer Service, Tourism, Gardening, Cooking, Arts, Graphic Design	Theoretical science, Entrepreneurship, Inventing, Technology, Architecture.	Marketing, Teaching, Healing, Counseling, Writing, Design.
Archetype	Warrior	King	Magician	Lover
Famous Examples	Bill Gates, General Patton, Lance Armstrong, George Washington, Serena Williams, Michael Jordan, Grep Popovich	Mother Theresa, Dr. Oz, Michael Jackson, Jackie Kennedy-Onnasis, Beyonce, Lebron James, Gordie Howe, Prince Harry	Steve Jobs, Albert Einstein, Walt Disney, Elon Musk, Whoopi Goldberg, Eckhart Tolle, JFK, Gordon Ramsey, Mark Cuban	Gandhi, M.L. King, Abraham Lincoln, Dr. Seuss, Tony Robbins, Bob Dylan, Dolly Parton, Tiger Woods

Next, we will look at how each of the functions combines not with each other, but with the attitudes of introversion and extraversion to create function-attitudes.

Typological Hemispheres and Meridians

An equally interesting geometrical shape to look at the polarities in the personality with is that of a globe. The equator is the horizontal ring that is intersected by the four functions of consciousness. It separates the globe into two halves. The upper half is Extraverted and the lower half Introverted.

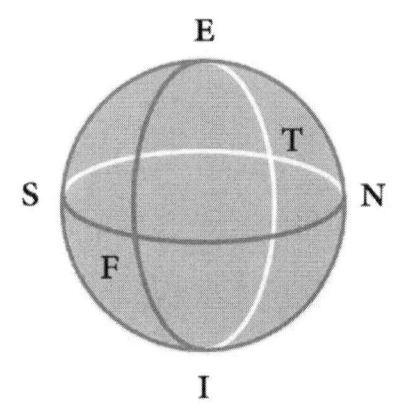

The meridians that run North-South (or E-I) represent what are called function-attitudes. A function-attitude is a process, a movement of energy, that runs from the North pole (Extraversion) to the South pole (Introversion) and vice versa. There are four meridians, one for each function of consciousness. Each function can further be divided into an Extraverted and an Introverted function-attitude making eight function-attitudes in total.

In chapter 10 of *Psychological Types* Jung calls each function-attitude a type. In the next table they are grouped per meridian with a description by Jung.

IF	Introverted Feeling	*Still waters run deep... their feelings are intensive rather than extensive. They develop depth.* (Jung, CW 6, § 641)
EF	Extraverted Feeling	*Feelings harmonize with objective situations and general values* (Jung, CW 6, § 597)
IS	Introverted Sensation	*Apprehends the background of the physical world rather than its surface.* (Jung, CW 6, § 649)
ES	Extraverted Sensation	*Life is an accumulation of actual experiences of concrete objects.* (Jung, CW 6, § 606)
IT	Introverted Thinking	*It formulates questions and creates theories, it opens up new prospects and insights...* (Jung, CW 6, § 628)
ET	Extraverted Thinking	*Makes activities dependent on intellectual conclusions... elevates... an objectively oriented intellectual formula, into the ruling principle not only for himself but for his whole environment.* (Jung, CW 6, § 585)
IN	Introverted Intuition	*Images represent possible views of the world which may give life a new potential* (Jung, CW 6, § 658)
EN	Extraverted Intuition	*Intuition tries to apprehend the widest range of possibilities, since only through envisioning possibilities is intuition fully satisfied.* (Jung, CW6, § 612)

These function-attitudes are psychological processes, not quite types yet. Just like the functions, the function-attitudes work in pairs and thus make up a type. A type is a pattern that is consistent in its characteristics. What types are we will see next when we switch back from to the double pyramid as our model for the personality.

A Typological Trinity: The Eight Triangular Sides of the Octahedron

Now that we understand the base of the double pyramid let us look at the lateral faces, or triangles, of both pyramids.

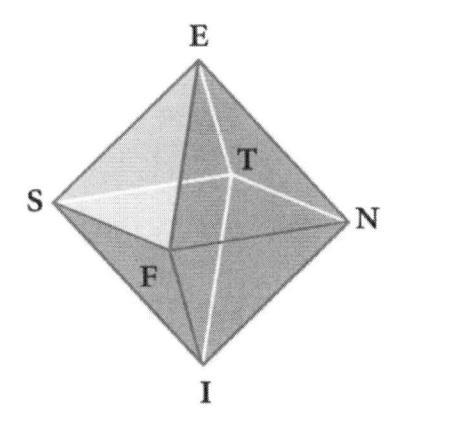

Each triangular face of the octahedron represents a typological entity. The base of each of the triangles is a temperament which can either find an introverted or extraverted expression. All four functions meet at the introverted and extraverted apex forming the following 8 combinations or types:

Type	Role	Qualities
IST	Investigator	Reflective, concrete and logical
ISF	Caretaker	Reflective, concrete and personal
INT	Architect	Reflective, imaginative and logical
INF	Dreamer	Reflective, imaginative and personal
EST	Operator	(Inter)active, concrete and logical
ESF	Host	(Inter)active, concrete and personal
ENT	Innovator	(Inter)active, imaginative and logical
ENF	Inspirer	(Inter)active, imaginative and personal

So far, the insights we have gained from the octahedron are that there are four temperaments represented by cross-sections of the base, and eight personality types represented by triangles (the lateral faces of the pyramid).

Range of Consciousness

Your type is determined by your preference for function and attitude. This does not mean, however, that you are one of sixteen types. You have a range. The range of consciousness is like the reach of the sun shining on the earth; it covers half of it. Sure, there is the spot on the globe that is directly under the sun, but the reach of the sun is half the globe. It is the same with you. When you do your self-assessment, and a four-letter code rolls out, that is your sweet spot, the place directly under the sun. However, you have conscious control over half the temperaments, half the types and half the sub-types. This does not necessarily mean that they are all well developed and differentiated, but there is conscious control.

Which two temperaments you have access to is determined by your dominant function. Suppose someone's dominant temperament is ST (Sensation-Thinking). It is important to know which function comes first (the dominant function) and which one comes second. If Thinking is dominant (and since Thinking is a judging function), we add a J to arrive at STJ. If Sensation is dominant, we add P to arrive at ISTP, since Sensation is a perceiving function. If Sensation is dominant, the other temperament is SF. There are eight possible combinations based on order of preference for each of the functions (1, 2, 3 and 4).

THE POWER OF POLARITIES

Type	1	2	3	4	Temperaments	Description
STP	S	T	F	N	ST + SF	Helping Technician
STJ	T	S	N	F	ST + NT	Inventive Technician
NTP	N	T	F	S	NT + NF	Visionary Inventor
NTJ	T	N	S	F	NT + ST	Technical Inventor
SFP	S	F	T	N	SF + ST	Technical Helper
SFJ	F	S	N	T	SF + NF	Visionary Helper
NFP	N	F	T	S	NF + NT	Inventive Visionary
NFJ	F	N	S	T	NF + SF	Helping Visionary

THE POWER OF POLARITIES

Moreover, each of these two temperaments can be both introverted and extraverted, giving rise to the following range of conscious types and roles. In the table below they are ranked 1-4 with the first one being most conscious and the fourth the least conscious.

16 Sub-Types	Conscious Types 1	2	3	4	Conscious Roles 1	2	3	4
ISTP	IST	EST	ISF	ESF	Investigator	Operator	Caretaker	Host
ISTJ	IST	EST	INT	ENT	Investigator	Operator	Architect	Innovator
ESTP	EST	IST	ESF	ISF	Operator	Investigator	Host	Caretaker
ESTJ	EST	IST	ENT	INT	Operator	Investigator	Innovator	Architect
INTP	INT	ENT	INF	ENF	Architect	Innovator	Dreamer	Inspirer
INTJ	INT	ENT	IST	EST	Architect	Innovator	Investigator	Operator
ENTP	ENT	INT	ENF	INF	Innovator	Architect	Inspirer	Dreamer
ENTJ	ENT	INT	EST	IST	Innovator	Architect	Operator	Investigator
INFP	INF	ENF	INT	ENT	Dreamer	Inspirer	Architect	Innovator
INFJ	INF	ENF	ISF	ESF	Dreamer	Inspirer	Caretaker	Host
ENFP	ENF	INF	ENT	INT	Inspirer	Dreamer	Innovator	Architect
ENFJ	ENF	INF	ESF	ISF	Inspirer	Dreamer	Host	Caretaker
ISFP	ISF	ESF	IST	EST	Caretaker	Host	Investigator	Operator
ISFJ	ISF	ESF	INF	ENF	Caretaker	Host	Dreamer	Inspirer
ESFP	ESF	ISF	EST	IST	Host	Caretaker	Operator	Investigator
ESFJ	ESF	ISF	ENF	INF	Host	Caretaker	Inspirer	Dreamer

138

THE POWER OF POLARITIES

The unconscious types and roles are listed in the table below. These types and roles that are more challenging to use because they are relatively unconscious. They typically lie in the Shadow of the personality. They are ranked 5-8 with the fifth being the least unconscious and the eight being the most unconscious or "inferior."

16 Sub-Types	Unconscious Types				Unconscious Roles			
	5	6	7	8	5	6	7	8
ISTP	INT	ENT	INF	ENF	Architect	Innovator	Dreamer	Inspirer
ISTJ	ISF	ESF	INF	ENF	Caretaker	Host	Dreamer	Inspirer
ESTP	ENT	INT	ENF	INF	Innovator	Architect	Inspirer	Dreamer
ESTJ	ESF	ISF	ENF	INF	Host	Caretaker	Inspirer	Dreamer
INTP	IST	EST	ISF	ESF	Investigator	Operator	Caretaker	Host
INTJ	INF	ENF	ISF	ESF	Dreamer	Inspirer	Caretaker	Host
ENTP	EST	IST	ESF	ISF	Operator	Investigator	Host	Caretaker
ENTJ	ENF	INF	ESF	ISF	Inspirer	Dreamer	Host	Caretaker
INFP	ISF	ESF	IST	EST	Caretaker	Host	Investigator	Operator
INFJ	INT	ENT	IST	EST	Architect	Innovator	Investigator	Operator
ENFP	ESF	ISF	EST	IST	Host	Caretaker	Operator	Investigator
ENFJ	ENT	INT	EST	IST	Innovator	Architect	Operator	Investigator
ISFP	INF	ENF	INT	ENT	Dreamer	Inspirer	Architect	Innovator
ISFJ	IST	EST	INT	ENT	Investigator	Operator	Architect	Innovator
ESFP	ENF	INF	ENT	INT	Inspirer	Dreamer	Innovator	Architect
ESFJ	EST	IST	ENT	INT	Operator	Investigator	Innovator	Architect

Benefits of this Model

This model has certain advantages in the practical application of Jung's theory:
- It distinguishes three levels abstraction which makes it possible to choose what level of abstraction to work with. Most personality models just have one or two. In this model, we can work with: 4 Temperaments, 8 Types, or 16 Sub-types.
- Besides having these different levels, the underlying hypothesis is that you can consciously access half of them. In other words, you are not one of sixteen types, but really eight of 16. Consequently, you have conscious control over half the temperaments (2) and half the types (4).
- If you are a Thinking type, INTJ, for instance, you can access both NT and ST temperaments. And even though there is a preference for introversion, you can also extravert both. In other words, you have access to four of eight types in the following order: INT, ENT, IST, and EST.
- I like to use an analogy with the sun here. The sun does not shed light on one point, or only 1/16th of the earth. It sheds light on half the earth. It is the same with the personality. Consciousness (light) can "illuminate" half the personality. This does more justice to someone's personality than narrowing it down to one of 16 (!) types.
- The octahedron is a meaningful three-dimensional model that people can use to reflect on their own personality. The same model can be viewed in a two-dimensional personality grid as well (and it is presented in the next chapter).
- In my experience, most people will tend to introvert and extravert their dominant function. They will still have their attitudinal preference, but with the dominant function, they can often shift to the other attitude. Typologically this means that the dominant function is the door through which consciousness can both enter and exit.

This model also has its limitations. An important limitation lies in the uniqueness of every individual. The way you use your personality will not just be typically different from others, but also uniquely different. The other limitation is that although this model is based on 30 years of experience and working with thousands of people and hundreds of teams, I would like to research the validity of the hypotheses put forward in this book to satisfy my own Sensation function.

What Problem Does This Model Solve?

How do you explain great human achievements, things that are achieved against all odds? Jung's theory provides us with a mental model not only for solving problems but for great human achievements. In my work with individuals and teams, I have discovered that great achievements are always grounded in the ability to use the power of polarities and cover all the bases of the personality. A simple exercise using the Apple company as an example can demonstrate this (bear in mind though, the same principles apply to individuals and teams).

Did Apple cover all the bases of the personality and use the power of polarities? The simple framework of the four temperaments can help us answer this question.

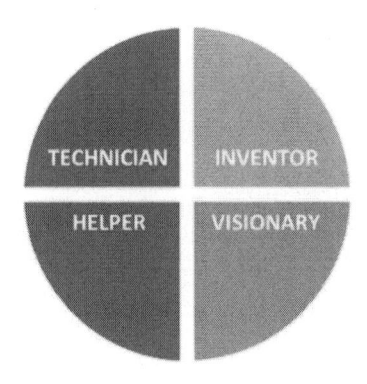

TEAL Temperament - Technician

Are Apple's products technically sound? Against the trend in the computer industry, Apple developed its hardware and software together for the sole reason of being able to make technically sound products. Their products have outperformed competitor's products in terms of both technical benchmarks and product lifetimes.

TERRACOTTA Temperament - Helper

This temperament is about helping people with their practical needs. Apple products have provided humankind with some life-changing practical tools. Just take the iPod as an example. From a CD-player with 12 songs to a thousand songs on a device the size of a deck of cards that fits in your pocket. The iPhone was a touchscreen iPod with a phone and email and internet in one. There had not been a device that could integrate all of these in one. And another thing the SF temperament likes are beauty of design. His collaboration with Jonathan Ive, Apple's chief designer, provided Apple with that. Design apparently has such a high priority at Apple, that engineering has to report to design, and not the other way around.

ORANGE Temperament - Visionary

The young Steve Jobs was driven by the following vision:

> *I read a study that measured the efficiency of locomotion for various species on the planet. The condor used the least energy to move a kilometer. Humans came in with a rather unimpressive showing about a third of the way down the list... That didn't look so good, but then someone at Scientific American had the insight to test the efficiency of locomotion for a man on a bicycle and a man on a bicycle blew the condor away. That's what a computer is to me: the computer is the most remarkable tool that we've ever come up with. It's the equivalent of a bicycle for our minds.*

So he set out to create technology that would be like a bicycle for the mind.

TURQUOISE Temperament - Inventor

Apple has thrived on innovation. From the first personal computer with a screen and a keyboard (1976) to the MacIntosh (1984), the iPod (2001), iPhone (2007) and iPad (2010). And in the process, they reinvented the music industry. We have gotten so used to these products that we have forgotten that many thought they would fail. Steve Ballmer, the former CEO of Microsoft said about the iPhone, *"There is no chance that the iPhone is going to get any significant market share. No chance."* A sign of true innovation is that it is at first met skepticism but succeeds despite it.

In every one of these four arenas', Apple has outperformed the market to become the company with the highest stock exchange value. Steve Jobs intuitively knew how to do this. At the same time, he was a man with many limitations. The Red Feeling function was his inferior function and it caused quite some havoc in his personal life and in his relationships with his colleagues. But this he got right. In his second term at Apple, he also figured out how important collaboration is. It is only through collaboration that you can cover all bases of the personality. No one person can cover them on their own. In a 2003 episode of 60 Minutes he said:

My model for business is The Beatles. They were four guys who kept each other kind of negative tendencies in check. They balanced each other and the total was greater than the sum of the parts. That's how I see business: great things in business are never done by one person, they're done by a team of people.

Apple's continued success since Steve Job's death in 2011 will depend on its ability to continue to outperform the market in these four arenas'. Artificial Intelligence (AI) is the new kid on the block that will change the global economy significantly for the next decades. The question is, can Apple successfully integrate this in all four arenas'?

Next chapter: practical and color-coded tools to work with.

CHAPTER 11

TEMPERAMENT, TYPE, AND COLOR

Since colour occupies so important a place in the series of elementary phenomena... we shall not be surprised to find that its effects are at all times decided and significant, and that they are immediately associated with the emotions of the mind.

~ Johann W. von Goethe, Theory of Colours, 1840

In the previous chapter, we learned that the perceiving and judging functions that form the base of the double pyramid work together in pairs. Each of these combinations, each of these pairs produces a temperament in the personality, a set of values, needs, interests, and traits that are "natural" to it and quite different from each other.

In 1985, Edward de Bono first introduced the concept of using colors (the "Six Thinking Hats ") to designate particular thought patterns. He used colors to more effectively approach issues and challenges (either individually or within a group) by giving them each a designated role.

Since then countless people and organizations have followed his example of using colors to identify various kinds of qualities. The reason for this is that colors are effective metaphors and provide people with a more illustrative language.

In the same way, we can use colors to designate the fundamental pairs of the perceiving and judging polarities in the personality.

		Perceiving	
		What is (S)	*What could be* (N)
Judging	*Logical impact* (T)	Teal: Logical and matter-of-fact	Turquoise: Logical and ingenious
	Personal impact (F)	Terracotta: Personal and caring	Orange: Personal and insightful

A Two-Dimensional Personality Grid

A horizontal or two-dimensional depiction of the three-dimensional octahedron emerged one evening from my experimentation with the octahedron. In my imagination, I opened it at the Extraversion (E) apex and unfolded it in four directions. The result, after I made a drawing on paper, was the two-dimensional *Polarities of the*

Personality Grid™ below in which the functions are represented by red, blue, yellow, and green, and the Four Temperaments by teal, turquoise, orange, and terracotta. The eight types are found within the temperament quadrant. In the corners of each quadrant are the letters representing the sixteen sub-types.

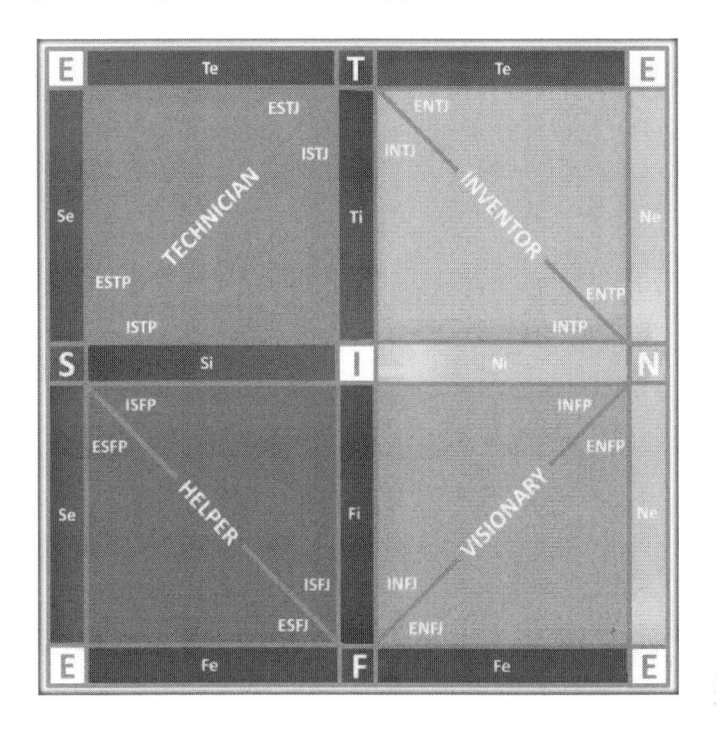

ST – Technician – Teal Temperament: Logical and Matter-of-Fact

ST (Temperament) types are skilled in working with practical, tangible things, and information. They like to make and manage things that are logical in nature and based on the law of cause and effect. They are focused on efficiency and doing whatever works, pays off, or is the shortest path to the goal. They like doing things "by the book" and will adhere to rules and regulations unless they believe there is a better way. They like to work hard and use tools to be efficient, are unusually self-disciplined and good at controlling themselves and their environment.

Famous examples: Bill Gates, General Patton, Lance Armstrong, George Washington, Serena Williams, Michael Jordan, Grep Popovich, Jack Welch, Peyton Manning, Thomas Edison.

SF – Helper – Terracotta Temperament: Personal and Caring
SF (Temperament) types are attached to the way things are and have always been. They are conscientious, follow the rules, respect and protect the rights of others, and expect their rights to be respected and protected as well. Such individuals value tradition and take good care of material possessions, themselves, and others. They like to provide safety, security, and material well-being to people in general, but especially to those they feel need it. There is usually a strong personal loyalty and commitment to a thing, cause, or person.

Famous examples: Mother Theresa, Dr. Oz, Michael Jackson, Jackie Kennedy-Onnasis, Beyonce, Lebron James, Gordie Howe, Prince Harry.

NF – Visionary – Orange Temperament: Personal and Insightful
NF (Temperament) types believe in ideas that will make the world a better place. They are usually able to imagine or even dream these ideas. They tend to nourish them until they can be realized, at which point the next idea is incubated. There is an intense desire to connect with others harmoniously and create "a new world" for humankind. They strive to discover unity in diversity, believing every being is connected, no matter the differences of form and shape. They conceive the world to be a place where ethical, peaceful, hopeful, and positive change can and will happen, and where conflict will finally end.

Famous examples: Gandhi, M.L. King, Abraham Lincoln, Dr. Seuss, Tony Robbins, Bob Dylan, Dolly Parton, Tiger Woods, The Beatles.

NT – Inventor – Turquoise Temperament: Logical and Ingenious

NT (Temperament) types like to investigate new problems and intriguing ideas using their vivid imagination and logical mind. They always strive for effectiveness and for improving the system through creativity (with big steps, not little ones). They tend to ignore the status quo, and if dissatisfied enough will challenge it with strong arguments. They can visualize the future state of things and are driven by a desire to bring the future into actuality.

Famous examples: Steve Jobs, Albert Einstein, Walt Disney, Elon Musk, Whoopi Goldberg, Eckhart Tolle, JFK, Gordon Ramsey, Mark Cuban, Nikola Tesla.

The qualities of the function couples or "Temperaments" of the personality are sometimes more easily recognized by looking at their relative strengths and weaknesses. The weaknesses appear when the personality loses its balance under stress, and the temperaments become overextended.

Strengths

Disciplined	Original
Precise	Purposeful
Practical	Independent
Efficient	Effective
Competitive	Bold
Supportive	Idealistic
Kind	Encouraging
Dependable	Holistic
Dedicated	Inspiring
Caring	Meaningful

Weakness under Stress

Controlling	Unrealistic
Nitpicking	Detached
Risk-averse	Argumentative
Calculating	Dominant
Ruthless	Narcissistic
Worried	Chaotic
Complaining	Inauthentic
Withdrawn	Codependent
Resentful	Flighty
Smothering	Insecure

Types as Triangles

As discussed earlier the Four Temperaments find their introverted or extraverted expression in the triangular sides of the octahedron. The triangles are named, colored, and described below. The triangles that point upwards are the extraverted types; the triangles pointing downwards are the introverted types.

EST OPERATOR — Outward-oriented and active. Direct and practical experience of the tangible world. Focuses on the here and now. Enjoys and responds quickly to sensory information and contact in the outer world. All actions are guided by impersonally focusing on the task at hand in a bold, precise, decisive, and commanding way. Likes to establish order in the outer world with rules, laws or procedures.

INVESTIGATOR IST — Inward and reflective. Likes to find, store, order, analyze, and reflect on all kinds of facts and information, with the intention of using this information in the future to solve problems or find logical truths and theoretical constructs.

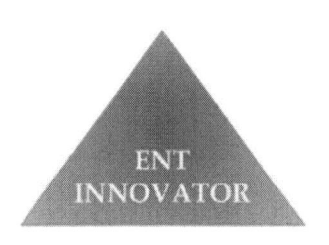

ENT INNOVATOR — Outward-oriented and open to new possibilities in the outer world. A rebel with a cause who, dissatisfied with the status quo, wants to challenge it. Sees potentials, options, and what is not yet visible to others. Will take bold risks or start a new adventure with great energy, believing in creating the future now.

ARCHITECT INT

Inward-oriented and reflective. Focuses on discovering the deeper meaning or structure of something. Sees all the connections, especially logical ones, and can express this in the creation of new designs, inventions or scientific theories. Generates knowledge and wisdom for the (technological) advancement of mankind.

ESF CAREGIVER

Outward-oriented and interactive. Likes to create a positive, harmonious order in society, focusing on people and tangible reality. Likes interacting with, entertaining, and enjoying life intensely with others. Promotes positive relationships, is expressive and charming.

CARETAKER ISF

Inward-oriented and reflective. Focuses on concrete and specific facts stores them for future reference and applies them to the current situation. Has an intense desire to live according to inner, human values. Upholds these values intensely and unconditionally. Likes to take care of other people and objects, and treats them with great respect and loyalty.

ENF INSPIRER: Strong ideals, outward-oriented and interactive, focuses on exploring new possibilities and believes in a better future for humankind. Inspires and engages new people along the way with infectious enthusiasm.

POET INF: Inward-oriented and reflective. Focuses on imagining, developing and growing internal images and ideas into the most fabulous and comprehensive stories and dreams. These dreams are really visions that concern people and the meaning of life. They can be so intense and profound that they need to be nurtured inside before they can be externalized.

The Power of Perception: What Color is Your Sky?

The man was bent over his guitar, a shearsman of sorts. The day was green.
They said, "You have a blue guitar, you do not play things as they are."
The man replied, "Things as they are, are changed upon the blue guitar."
(Wallace Stevens, inspired by Picasso's The Blind Old Guitarist)

Whereas reality is in front of your eyes, the way you perceive and organize it is behind your eyes. It is there that your personality preferences filter and organize data. The remarkable result is that two people can disagree and yet both be right because there is no absolute measure of reality. The human condition is such that there is more that we don't know than we do. Leonardo da Vinci is supposed to have said, *"All our knowledge has its origin in our perceptions."* If this is true, it means that the more we perceive, the greater our knowledge of reality becomes. So, if we can enhance our perception, we see more, *and* we know more.

Two people can look at the same thing and see something different. Take this image, for example:

- Do you see the saxophone player?
- What does he look like?
- Do you see the woman?
- What does she look like?
- Can you see both?

This single image can be seen as both a saxophone player and a woman. The point here is, two people can both see something different, and both be right. They can disagree and both be right. As stated above, reality is not what is in front of our eyes, but what is behind them. It is not logical, but psychological.

If we can see both the saxophone player and the woman in the image, we know the object we are observing can be two things, not just one. To be able to see this, we must do some work. We have to be willing to examine our own and others' perceptions.

Our worldview is primarily determined by our temperament, i.e., the combination of a perceiving (S/N) and judging (T/F) function. There are four worldviews, and the good news is that two of those are relatively easy for us to access. Have a look below and decide which two temperaments tend to color your sky.

TEAL (Blue/Green) Temperament - Technician
People under the Teal Sky will look for hard, tangible facts and their logical order. They see the world as the result of cause and

effect, are highly technical, and are good at establishing rules and procedures. People with this worldview often like to practice law, engineering, or Western medicine. A good example is Bill Gates, with his determination to dominate office software through Microsoft. It is the most prevalent worldview in Europe and North America.

TERRACOTTA (Red/Green) Temperament - Helper
People under the Terracotta Sky people will engage with the practical side of reality and will be inclined to see how they affect people. They seek to organize the world in a way that meets human needs, and they strive to help and be of service to others. People with this worldview work in professions like nursing, childcare, education, and hospitality. This temperament is prevalent in certain Asian and South American countries.

ORANGE (Red/Yellow) Temperament - Visionary
People under the Orange Sky are not oriented towards tangible facts but towards intangible human principles like love, personal growth, and human rights. They seek to organize the world in ways that help people fulfill their potential. They are interested in creating a new vision or narrative for humanity, and can express this poetically, like Martin Luther King in his "I Have a Dream" speech or Bob Dylan in a song like *The Times They Are A-Changin'*. People with this worldview can be found in more idealistic professions like psychology, counseling, religious leadership, writing, poetry, and movies.

TURQUOISE (Blue/Yellow) Temperament - Inventor
People under the Turquoise Sky are interested in "thought experiments" through which they discover new and exciting ideas that will change the world. They like to make scientific discoveries, or create inventions, innovations, new designs and architectures. People with this worldview like to make the future happen, like Steve Jobs in technology, Albert Einstein in physics, or Frank Lloyd Wright in architecture.

Under each of these four color skies, things look very different. Let's say you want to build a new house. Teal will insist it is done according to all technical specification, on time and within budget. Turquoise will want to implement new technologies and new designs, something the Teal will find too risky. Terracotta will want to focus on the people that will live in the house and their needs. And Orange will be dreaming of the most marvelous designs, which are more like air castles than real homes.

And yet, when these four skies come together, a creative process takes place with unusual results. Frank Lloyd Wright, the great American architect, was able to integrate all four views and in the process "changed the way we build and live." I discovered this when I visited the Frank Lloyd Wright Museum in Oak Park near Chicago on a business trip with a colleague. Before that trip, I only knew his name from the Simon & Garfunkel song. That visit opened my eyes to his great architectural achievements. Allow me to explain how he did this from the perspective of each color sky.

ORANGE Temperament - Visionary

As an architect, Wright had a vision of harmony between a structure and its environment. He pioneered the Prairie Style homes, which were buildings with a long, low, and open floor plan. They had long, low-pitched roofs that fit in the American prairie landscape (unlike the "boxes" that the Victorian houses looked like). Abstract forms from nature would decorate the interior. Wright said about his work:

> *The mission of an architect is to help people understand how to make life more beautiful, the world a better one for living in, and to give reason, rhyme, and meaning to life.*

1901 Article by Frank Lloyd Wright in the "Ladies Home Journal"

TURQUOISE Temperament - Inventor

Wright's designs were among the most innovative of his era. He experimented with geometric shapes like no architect before and since him. He was always embracing new technologies, pushing the boundaries in his field. The Johnson Wax Headquarters in Racine, Wisconsin is a good example of innovation in office building design. It was the first building to use Pyrex glass tubing, and there were no windows in the walls. All the light came from the ceiling thanks to the use of revolutionary columns.

Work Area at the Johnson Wax Headquarters. (Source: Wikimedia)

TERRACOTTA Temperament - Helper

Wright's designs are known for the attention to detail on the interior of a home. He wanted to make sure every human need was accommodated for. He gave considerable thought to all the processes that take place in a home, like meals, sitting together in a central space like a dining room and storage. For this, he would design built in cabinets, seating, tables, and light fixtures. He also gave attention to all the details of lighting, heating, and plumbing.

Fallingwater Residence Sitting Area (Source: Wikimedia)

TEAL Temperament - Technician

This was not the strongest element of Wright's work. He would often clash with construction contractors on the structural components of the building. Also, his structures were seldom realized on time and within budget, something that is very important under the Teal Sky of the Technician. One of his most famous residences, "Fallingwater" in rural Pennsylvania, was budgeted at $35,000 while the final cost was $155,000. More than four times the original price. It is fair to say that in working with Wright there was never a dull moment and his clients had to put up with a lot. But they put up with it because they knew Wright would build them something extraordinary that would be part of their legacy. At the same time, many clients decided against engaging Wright. From the more than 1,000 structures he designed only about half were completed.

After his death in 1959, Frank Lloyd Wright has received ample recognition for his work. Fallingwater was named "Building of the Century" in 2000. Other buildings like the Guggenheim Museum and the Johnson Wax Building also ended high on that list.

CHAPTER 12

THE POWER OF PURPOSE

The book on types yielded the insight that every judgment made by an individual is conditioned by his personality type and that every point of view is necessarily relative. This raised the question of the unity which must compensate this diversity...

~ C.G. Jung, 1989, Chapter VII: The Work

My general formula for my students is "Follow your bliss." Find where it is, and don't be afraid to follow it.

~ Joseph Campbell, The Power of Myth, 1988, p. 120

Who are we if we do not know our center? There has never been, nor will there ever be another you. There is a life force which is you, which enters the world through you, and only you can give expression to it. Your center is where you find your purpose and where your life becomes a unique and authentic act of being and service to humankind.

What has surprised me in this work is that this is most clearly understood by those who have witnessed the devastation of war. I have often wondered why soldiers struggle to reintegrate into civilian life and long to be back in the war they just survived. Perhaps I am sensitive to this issue because my grandfather, Col. Dwight Kuhns, was in the U.S. Army Medical Corps and served in both World War II and the Korean War. We were very close, and he passed away a long time ago, so I cannot ask him, but I have a hunch that in his day he understood the meaning of this chapter very well. Whatever the reason for my interest may be, I found the answer in this: *very few have had a stronger experience of purpose and community than those who have served their country in war.*

In his book *Through our Eyes* (2008), Jesse Odom, a Marine infantryman who fought in Baghdad, recounts the following:

> *The most devastating perpetual trauma I had to overcome was civilian transition… I know the changes I see in myself are not a result of the war in Iraq. Even though those memories are still there and are traumatic, it goes much deeper than that. The changes are the result of a man who wishes he was at war.*

Karl Marlantes, a decorated Marine veteran of the Vietnam war, in his book *What It Is Like to Go to War* (2012), confirms that it is hard for veterans to adjust to civilian life. He writes that it is like *"asking St. John of the Cross to be happy flipping burgers at McDonald's after he's left the monastery."*

The documentary *Restrepo* (2010) chronicles the lives of soldiers in a platoon in Afghanistan from their deployment to their return home. Sebastian Junger, one of the directors, stated in an interview:

> *Soldiers come back from a very unified experience where no one cares if you're gay or straight, Republican or Democrat, Harvard educated, or your dad's in prison. No one cares, right? And then you come back to America where we're [a] completely politically divided and economically*

and racially divided society, and I think it's appalling to soldiers who encounter that back home when it didn't exist in the front lines.
(Chang, et al., 2014)

Fortunately, there are now organizations that give veterans a renewed sense of purpose, like *Team Rubicon* and *Squad Bay*. But that is not enough; we have an opportunity to learn from our veterans and their experiences as a society. They know what it is like to be purpose and community driven and to look past the prejudices that divide people.

Having a sense of purpose, unity, and community is what young men returning from war miss most. War provided them with that. Victor Frankl was an Austrian psychiatrist who survived Auschwitz. The human horrors he experienced there also provided him with insight. In *Man's Search for Meaning* (1984) he writes: *"Life is never made unbearable by circumstances, but only by lack of meaning and purpose"* and *"Those who have a 'why' to live, can bear with almost any 'how'."*

It is most regrettable that in our society the strongest experience of this is in war. Purpose can be found in so many other areas of life: one's professional life, a love relationship or in a particular hardship one has to face. A sense of meaning is not achieved by blindly accepting one's fate, but by formulating an individual response to it from within, from one's own unique center. In the Foreword to Frankl's book, Harold Kushner (author of *When Bad Things Happen to Good People*, 2007) writes:

Forces beyond your control can take away everything you possess except one thing, your freedom to choose how you will respond to the situation. You cannot control what happens to you in life, but you can always control what you will feel and do about what happens to you.

The experience of purpose and unity with oneself and others is something that is very powerful and within everyone's ability to create and experience. War and combat are not necessary prerequisites. Also, if we had more purpose and community in our society, it would be easier for veterans to reintegrate.

Finding a common purpose is also the fundamental principle behind developing high- performance teams. It is the only way in which individual personality differences can be united for positive impact. The only other way to unite people is fear, but the problem with fear is that it unites people *against* something instead of *for* something positive that they believe in.

As an individual, you can find a sense of purpose by asking yourself:
- What kind of world would I like to create? What change would I like to see?
- What do I care about so deeply that I will do almost anything to change it?
- What could I do to make these changes happen?
- What unique abilities do I possess that could make a difference in this respect?

Once you find your purpose, you can experience its power by following Gandhi's advice: *"Be the change you want to see in the world."* That is ultimately the most fulfilling venture any of us can undertake.

Man is Most Nearly himself, When He Achieves the Seriousness of a Child at Play - Heraclitus

One of the best criteria I know to establish whether someone is working in the area of their passion is if they "achieve the seriousness of a child at play." A child at play is curious, innocent, excited and completely devoted to that one thing it is busy with. One of the qualities that made Einstein such a great scientist was his insatiable curiosity to understand the natural world. Just like Carl

Jung was driven by an insatiable curiosity to understand the human psyche. With these men, it was an almost childlike curiosity, intense and pure. This is the archetype of the inner child.

The child in us, the child we always were and still are, has three essential qualities: curiosity, excitement, and innocence. Curiosity is like thirst or hunger. It drives you forward. Excitement is like the fire in the belly. And innocence assumes nothing, is always open to something new or different.

If we allow ourselves to be led by our curiosity, excitement, and innocence, we discover our passion. And passion is crucial to our purpose, our calling. The thing you are passionate about it the thing you would love doing the rest of your life, no matter how hard it is. If we target our passion with our unique ability (or superpower) and put this at the service of something greater than ourselves, a contribution to the world, we have found our purpose.

We can state this principle in an equation:

$$Purpose = Superpower \times Passion \times Service$$

The nature of a mathematical equation like this is that if one of the factors of multiplication is 0, the value before the equal sign becomes 0. For example, if you have passion and want to be of service, but you do not know your superpower, there is no purpose. Suppose that Passion is a 10 and Service is a 10, but Superpower is unknown and unused: Purpose = $0 \times 10 \times 10 = 0$

The other caveat with an equation like this is that there has to be alignment in order to multiply. For example, if I am passionate about chess but do not have chess superpowers, it will not work. Similarly, if I do have the superpower and passion for playing chess but do this strictly for personal gain, I won't experience purpose.

The consequences of this become apparent if you look at a large corporation like Enron (these principles are the same whether you look at individuals, teams or organizations). Enron's rise and fall have been the subject of many articles and even a movie. The storyline is familiar: they were smart guys who were passionate about their company but selfish and greedy, which led to their downfall. Putting yourself in the service of others keeps you on a straight and narrow moral path. If the Enron leadership had prioritized their clients' interests, would they have illegally shut down pipelines to create shortages (even black-outs) in order to raise their energy prices?

An example of alignment is Apple, whose founders Steve Jobs and Steve Wozniak had superpowers that were applicable to their passion for computers which they built to "delight customers." Another interesting fact is that Apple did not pay a shareholder dividend from 1995 until 2011 when Steve Jobs passed away. Apple was and will hopefully continue to be devoted to serving its customers first, not its shareholders.

Aligning superpower, passion, and service is crucial to staying on track during the next step: execution. Execution of Purpose leads to legacy: leaving something behind of lasting value for humanity.

Making Your Mark: Execution of Purpose and Lasting Impact

Stephen Covey, the author of *The Seven Habits of Effective People* (2013), coined the phrase "Live, Love, Laugh and Leave a Legacy." Whether you are an individual, team or organization, this is the game you are in. When you live and work with a clear and aligned purpose, you live a life of love and joy. The great work of your life will be accomplished when you love what you do.

The next equation to consider is this one:

Legacy = Purpose x Execution

Execution is the test and fuel of purpose. It is the test because you will only be able to execute if your superpower, passion, and sense of service align. It is the fuel because execution develops and strengthens your superpower, passion, and commitment to service. The legacy diagram below shows how all the elements tie in together to have a lasting impact.

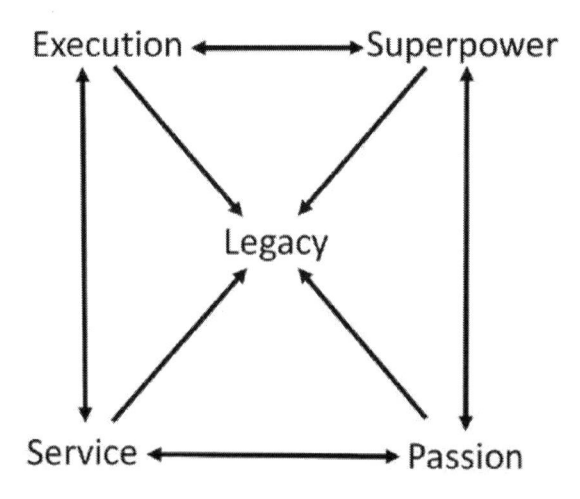

```
Execution ←――――→ Superpower
         ↘     ↗
          Legacy
         ↗     ↖
Service ←――――→ Passion
```

Successful athletes are a good example of how these elements work together to give them careers that last. Most players on the Olympic gold medal team of which I was the mental coach had a story that went like this:

> *When I was a young player there were other kids who were more talented than me. But they stopped coming to practice. I had so much passion for the game that I always showed up. And by the time I was 20, they were no longer around while I was among the best.*

Execution also means staying the course no matter what. There will be challenges, distractions, manipulations, conflicts, wrenches thrown in the works. This is where the adage *"Know Thyself"* becomes as important as knowing others. Using and balancing the polarities in your personality and those of others is the absolute key here. Thousands of years of human history prove this (as Carl Jung demonstrated: the first nine chapters in his book *Psychological Types* were about typological conflicts in history). An effective and powerful way of doing this is by defining values that represent the polarities in the personality.

Power of Values – Build Community

> *Your beliefs become your thoughts,*
> *Your thoughts become your words,*
> *Your words become your actions,*
> *Your actions become your habits,*
> *Your habits become your values,*
> *Your values become your destiny.*
> ~ Gandhi

When a purpose includes values, a sense of unity and community is created. The values are like "operating guidelines" for the individual or group, and they greatly aid the execution of the purpose. People get a sense of, "This is how we do things here. This is how we stick together in good times and bad. This is how we achieve amazing results." And the challenge is to stick to them, even in the most stressful conditions. In the end, living according to your values makes you valuable.

When I work with a team, I always let them choose and define four values. To harness the power of polarities, there must either be one value for each function, or one for each temperament. Here is an example: the purpose statement I developed for my consulting practice:

Vision   *A world where people discover the truths that give them life.*

Mission   *We facilitate teams in their transition to the next levels of awareness, collaboration, and performance.*

Values   *Practical Impact (ST – Teal Temperament – Technician)*
Innovation (NT – Turquoise Temperament – Inventor)
Service (ST – Terracotta Temperament – Helper)
Integrity (NF – Orange Temperament – Visionary)

The values or "operating principles" need some fleshing out to have a practical effect. Many organizations have official value statements that lack the clarity required for execution. In my workshops, I let the participants define their values using the following components:

- Tagline
- Definition
- Behavior

The following is a fleshed out example of the value of "Practical Impact" at Polarity Consulting:

Tagline	Practical Impact
Definition	Partner with clients to deliver learning solutions that enable their teams to accomplish the objectives that matter to them.
Behavior	• Provide a neutral, outside pair of eyes that see and ears that listen. • Bring focus and ask the questions that the situation requires. • Design and (if necessary) adapt a program to address the needs and objectives of a team as effectively as possible. • Transform the tension of conflict into positive outcomes for the team.

	- Ask that individual members of the team contribute to the team's purpose using their unique strengths. - Clarify what has been achieved, identify action items and next steps. - Remember that perfection is the enemy of the good and that good enough is good enough.

Note: It does not have to be this detailed, usually 3 or 4 behavior items is "good enough."

Solid values or "operating principles" will ensure an operational balance between all four temperaments, i.e., ensure all four temperaments are used and guide the resolution of conflicts. The whole set of values ensures that all the polarities in the personality are used and respected. One might think that values only apply to teams and organizations, but they are just as valid and important on an individual level. There is a little secret here: even if you have not defined values for yourself yet, you already have them. Everyone has certain "principles," and if they are violated, they get upset. They belong on paper where you can reflect on them and improve them where wanted or needed.

We are not there yet. What objectives will we direct our actions towards during the execution phase?

Setting Objectives = Taking Aim

Take dead aim at a spot on the fairway or green, refuse to allow any negative thought to enter your head and swing away...
(Harvey Penick, Hall of Fame golf coach from Austin, Texas)

Harvey Penick was a famous golf teacher. He noticed that when he asked players about their target before a golf swing, they did not aim at a particular point. He told them to pick a specific point and take dead aim.

What do you want to achieve? What achievements will be the highest expression of your purpose? Aim at these things as accurately as possible. Focus.

There are three levels of objectives:
- Outcome
- Performance
- Process

Outcome objectives are usually related to a period of a year. E.g. reach the Final Four, achieve 12% market share, realize a 20% profit margin. The problem with outcome objectives is that they usually depend on others and the environment you are in. Objectives that you can control are performance and process objectives. A performance objective is the demonstration of a certain skill or competence that has been developed through a process.

Take the example of the basketball team of country X. They have qualified for the Olympics and want to win a gold medal. During the qualifying games they performed poorly on free throws and they know they are going to have to improve in that area to win a gold medal. As a team they decide that every day after practice each player has to take a series of 30 free throws. In terms of types of objectives this means:
- *Outcome:* win a gold medal
- *Performance:* make more free throws
- *Process:* take 30 free throws individually after every training session.

There are many ways to identify and work with objectives; I found the following an effective method to identify them:
- Description
- Key Performance Indicator (KPI)
- Result (How do you know you have reached your objective?)

In the simplified example of country X's basketball team, a set of objectives could like this.

Outcome Objective

Description	Win a gold medal at the 2020 Tokyo Olympics
KPI	# of medals
Result	1 Gold

Performance Objective

Description	Improve free throw shooting as a team
KPI	% of free throws made in each game
Result	Greater than 80%

Process Objective

Description	Players take free throws daily after practice
KPI	# of free throws
Result	30

As stated before, the challenge with an outcome oriented objective is that the achievement is beyond your control. On a given day the other team simply can be better. A good way to approach this problem is to distinguish between a realistic result and an aspirational result. The aspirational result for an Olympic team could be a gold medal. A realistic result could be to reach the semi-finals. In the event that even the realistic result is not achieved, this is to be interpreted as feedback that something needs to change and the process evaluated.

Another challenge can be managing and tracking all objectives. This can be quite laborious. It is advisable to apply the 80-20 rule (or Pareto Principle): 80% of the effects come from 20% of the causes. For example, in sales 20% of the customers are responsible for 80% of the revenue. In terms of objectives it means prioritizing for impact. Another approach can be to work on the objectives in phases.

Summary: Four Key Elements of a Purpose Statement

This covers the four essential elements of a purpose statement: Vision – Mission – Values – Objectives. You can add more depending on your situation and whether you are an individual, team, or organization. But you cannot do with less. The table below gives an overview of each element, which components are involved and what the key questions are to ask yourself.

Key Elements of a Purpose Statement

Element	Component	Key Question
Vision	Passion Service	What type of world do you want to help create?
Mission	Superpower	What will you do, what is your unique contribution in creating this desired world?
Values	Execution	How, according to which principles, will you operate to complete your mission and achieve your vision?
Objectives	Execution	What achievements will reflect your purpose?

The structure of a purpose statement is not fundamentally different for an individual, team or organization, but the answers are. I include below as an example a simplified statement for a tech company X (adapted from reality).

Example of a Purpose Statement for Tech Company X

Element	Formulation
Vision	We enhance the mobile productivity of every being on this planet by making 21st century computing power in the form of technology "X" available to everyone, everywhere.
Mission	We consistently provide a highly reliable and innovative product portfolio in technology "X" to our customers globally by investing in product development and quality management.
Values	*Leading Innovation* – Provide customers with strategically innovative products. *Customer First* – Exceed our customer's needs and expectations always. *Simply The Best* – We outperform our competition in marketing, development, production and managing demand of our product portfolio. *Engage Every Individual* – Everyone on our team commits to achieve our objectives and gets the support needed to do so.
Objectives	• Sales of $ X.- in the year 2020 with an operating profit > 20% • Net Promoter Score > 60% • Sales of Innovative Products (% of products sold under 3 years old) > 75% • Investment in R&D between 8-10% of revenue • Capex to sales ratio of 20-25%

A well-crafted statement is simple, compelling and energizes the whole. Ideally it fits on one page and elicits reactions like, "Finally I understand why I am doing this job, what our team is here for." Or, "I cannot wait to tell the others." Or an individual might say, "I finally know what I want to do with my life."

There is one more relevant detail concerning a purpose statement... You should craft it, draft it and commit to it as though it is for eternity. And at the same time agree to review, refine or adjust it regularly. There is no way to get it 100% right the first time, but you need to start somewhere with the best initial plan you can come up with. Good enough is good enough. Decide what direction you want to take and go, make it happen.

A purpose statement is a high-level plan that is committed to by everyone involved and guides their actions every day. There is such power in commitment to direction and action. Or as the 19th century German philosopher and statesman Goethe wrote:

Until one is committed, there is hesitancy, the chance to draw back, always ineffectiveness. Concerning all acts of initiative and creation, there is one elementary truth the ignorance of which kills countless ideas and splendid plans: that the moment one definitely commits oneself, then providence moves too... Whatever you can do or dream you can, begin it. Boldness has genius, power and magic in it. Begin it now.

Chapter 13

Teamology - The Power of Polarities in Practice

Individual commitment to a group effort--that is what makes a team work, a company work, a society work, a civilization work.

~ Vince Lombardi, American football coach

We can think of a team as the cornerstone of an organization, much like we think of the family as the cornerstone of society. More than anything, it shapes the attitude, ambitions, values, and performance of the members of a team. Organizations thrive when their people thrive. Most people thrive in teams. They are the fundamental unit of human collaboration. There also is no unit of people in which the Power of Polarities can be felt so strongly. It can make or break a team.

When a team is dysfunctional, the result is not only low performance but also negativity and emotional tension, which reinforce the downward spiral in performance. The output of a well-functioning team is not just significantly higher than that of a group of individuals: it is exponentially higher. At least that is my experience from working with hundreds of teams. But don't just take my word for it!

Convincing Evidence from a Stanford Engineering Professor

There is some very convincing quantitative evidence from the book this chapter is named after. In 2008, Doug Wilde, a professor at the Department of Mechanical Engineering at Stanford University, published a remarkable book called *Teamology*. In it, he describes how his department used Jungian typology to form and organize effective problem-solving teams.

Starting in 1991, individual members of engineering teams were selected on the basis of typological diversity. Every member had to have different personality preferences. With all the polarities present, their power could be accessed. In his book Wilde reports that the results were spectacular.

In the thirteen years preceding the use of teamology in his department, 27% of the student teams won the Lincoln Design Awards competition they entered. After 9 years of teamology this percentage was 73%. The increase in award-winning performance was staggering. It meant that three-quarters of the students were performing at the level previously attained by only one quarter. There was only one bad year when the results dropped back to 25%. That was the year professor Wilde was absent, and teamology was not employed.

This method was also applied in 2007 at the Shanghai Jiao-Tong University in China with similar results. Wilde writes:

Remarkably, their forty nominal quintets almost universally generated projects of the same prize-quality as the Stanford Sophomore Seminar teams. This was a massive validation of the new teamology.
(Wilde, 2008, Chapter 6: Innovation and Errors)

How is something like this possible? Wilde:

The basic idea is to have every team possess among its members the full range of problem-solving approaches available to the human race. People who individually have only a few problem-solving strategies can pool these in a good team to make it overcome any obstacle it encounters.
(Wilde, 2008, Preface)

How these teams were formed differed from the way most teams are formed. The most important criteria became diversity of personality. Conformity, which is probably the most habitual way of forming teams, was avoided. In typology, the drive towards conformity is called the "Be like me" disorder. You see it in hiring processes everywhere. What this study shows is how it actually weakens team performance.

This type of team formation does come with a challenge: how to get the diverse members of a team to collaborate effectively. Wilde refers to this as "Organizing the team." Without this, the approach probably would not have worked as well. He used the Meyers-Briggs Type Indicator (MBTI), the most widely used instrument for Jungian type, not only to select the teams but also to conduct workshops and define team roles. Wilde writes:

The MBTI generates in team members the self-awareness and tolerance of different points of view needed in a cognitively diverse team... Different people see things differently, and it is possible to disagree without being disagreeable.
(Wilde, 2008, Chapter 4: Organizing a Team)

I couldn't agree more!

Polarity Team Building Methodology

For the past fifteen years, I have focused on building teams using Jungian Typology, and I want to share the approach I have developed and have found to be so incredibly effective.

The framework that all workshops follow to create a team as strong as a "table with four legs" is this:

1. *Know yourself* - Your strengths and limitations
2. *Understand others* - Value differences
3. *Find your purpose* - It is waiting to be discovered
4. *Execute* - Make your mark

Before we dive into examples and programs, there is one important condition for optimizing a team's performance. Whether you are an organization or a sports team, I have experienced the following to be true:

1. The fish rots from the head down.
2. As above, so below.

If we take a sports team as an example, when there are dysfunction, conflict, and strife in the coaching staff, this is transmitted to the players. It will make it very hard for the team to unify and become high-performing. When the coaching staff is a coherent, well-performing team, it also becomes much, much easier for the players to become a coherent, well-performing team.

I live in Austin, Texas close to the UT Longhorn Football Stadium where Charlie Strong was fired as a coach in November 2016. He was a great recruiter and someone the players loved. Throughout his career at both the University of Louisville and the University of Texas problems with his staff have been his Achilles' heel. He often had to make changes to his staff midseason. It is a good example of how hard it is to create a winning team if you do not have a winning coaching staff. With hindsight, the football program would have benefited, and his dismissal as a coach possibly avoided, had there been a focus on building the coaching staff into a strong team first.

So, when I work with a sports team, I work with the coaching staff and players separately at first. I do the same with the executive team or management team of a business unit. When they go through the process of becoming a team, the rest of the business unit follows their lead.

When it comes to programs, there are a lot of options. With sports teams, I do a series of relatively short interventions of 2-3 hours. That is usually the amount of time a practice takes, and they are geared to be able to focus for that amount of time.

The following is an example of an effective program for a two-day team retreat, but be aware it can be split into a series of shorter interventions as well. For participants it is hard work but it gives a lot of energy as well. It follows the structure of the "table with four legs" framework above.

DAY 1

What?	*Why?*
Opening, Welcome & Introductions	Introduce delegates to each other, to the program, and to the facilitators
Card Game	Ice Breaker and connecting with each other
Objectives, Program & Ground rules	Set the pace for the day
Power of Perception	- Understand how our perception is filtered by the concepts and paradigms we live with - We can change what we know by changing our perception

Elements of the Personality	- Understand the four basic Temperaments of the personality - Understand the stress behaviors of each Temperament
Jungian Personality Preferences	- Understand what is a personality preference and that there is no good or bad - Introversion vs: Extraversion - Thinking vs: Feeling - Sensing vs: Intuition
BREAK	
8 Main Personality Types	- Understand how we move from four Temperaments to eight Types - Demonstrate how different types need each other - Demonstrate that each team needs different roles
Profiles and Team Constellation	- Understand profile text - Understand graphs and how they relate to personal life - See what your and others' strengths and weaknesses are - Learn to value differences
LUNCH	
Four Corner Exercise around <STRATEGIC THEME>	- Understand what each Temperament contributes to a strategic theme for your team
Feedback Exercise	- Giving and receiving feedback as a way of telling each other your perception of the truth, a true "Breakfast for Champions"
BREAK	

Common Mission/Purpose	- Create common purpose for the team - Make it a collaborative effort so that every individual contribution is included - Practice teamwork (set agenda, facilitate & timekeeping)
Evaluation of process so far followed by	- Recap the program - Make sure everyone is connected with the process
DINNER	
Continue work on common Mission/Purpose and formulate set of goals	- Pay specific attention to goal setting and metrics

DAY 2

What?	*Why?*
Recap of yesterday	- Ground the learning and the results from the first day - Ensure every participant is connected to the process
Presentation of Vision, Mission & Goals	- Create common understanding of Vision, Mission & Goals - Reflect on them and fine tune if necessary

Make a framework of values together, balanced over the Four Corners	- Collaboratively create a set of values
	- Ensure that there is balance in the values in terms of polarities and in terms of focus:
	    ○ Facts vs. Ideas
	    ○ Tasks vs. Relationships
	    ○ Inner vs. Outer orientation

Extend framework to include definitions	- Concretization of values - Make framework easy to implement

and behavior	• Create clarity and direction in teamwork
LUNCH	
Present values	• Common understanding • Fine tuning
Personal goal-setting exercise	• Ensure every participant will make a personal contribution to the team as a result of this workshop
Closing	• Wrap up loose ends • Ensure everyone is still connected to the process

Feedback is the Breakfast of Champions

Breakfast is the most important meal of the day. Without a good breakfast, you cannot get through the day. Likewise, without feedback, your team starves. It cannot adapt, it cannot improve and cannot get through the day.

Giving and receiving feedback is always a critical moment of change in the life of a team. It gets people out of the trenches and opens things up very quickly and effectively. A feedback session can be as short as an hour-and-a-half for a team of ten to fifteen people. Afterwards, there is a sense of relief, and you can feel the tensions have cleared. The atmosphere is like a bright blue sky after a heavy storm.

Objectives of feedback:
- To disclose your truth, to open yourself up to others. This is what builds chemistry and strong relationships in a team.
- To start a process of self-awareness, both for the giver and receiver of feedback.
- To set in motion meaningful and relevant change within the team in a respectful way.

The effects are huge. Things that have sometimes been kept under the table for years are finally expressed in a safe and respectful way. But the session has to be structured well. There are many feedback methods out there. I describe the structures I use below. They comprise a proven, highly effective and time-efficient approach that can be adapted to a given situation.

Positive vs. Constructive Feedback

It is important to give both types of feedback and to start with the Positive (this makes it much easier for the Constructive to be accepted later). Usually, we do not give someone positive feedback until they leave the team or organization. Or sometimes we even wait until the funeral service. Have you ever attended a funeral service and thought, "I wish this person had heard this while he was still alive."? What if they could have heard your truly heartfelt and specific positive feedback while you were still part of the team? It is very motivating to feel truly appreciated.

Constructive feedback (also called criticism) is given more readily, but not usually in a way people can accept and process for the benefit of the team and themselves. The whole point is letting each other know what behavior and actions you want to:
- Continue.
- Improve
- Stop
- Start

Setting the Stage for Feedback Sessions

Before you start giving each other feedback, you need to set the stage and "prime the feedback pump." I usually deliver the following introduction to feedback:

1. *Feedback is the "Breakfast of Champions."* Because even if only 1% is true you can use it to improve yourself.

2. *Feedback is Free!* You are free to speak your personal truth, and the receiver of feedback is free to do with it what they want.
3. *Feedback is a Human Right.* You have the right to know how others perceive you and to hear both their positive and constructive feedback.
4. *Feedback is a Gift.* When you receive feedback all you say is "Thank you." Just like when you receive a gift. Arguing about the truth of the feedback is irrelevant and disrespectful to the person giving you the feedback. When you receive a gift, do you question it? Do you discuss whether it is the right gift for you? The most important thing is to receive it and unpack it, even if you do not like it or completely disagree!
5. *Feedback is a personal interpretation of a situation.* It says more about the person giving the feedback than the person receiving it.

Each of these principles is important. My experience is that if you skip one, you are in for a tough session! I once worked with a leader who I noticed others in the organization feared. After I sat in on a meeting with him and his team, I decided to give him some feedback privately. I felt it was important because I observed a complete disconnect between him and his team, and nobody seemed to be aware of it.

After I gave him this feedback, he took some time to explain why I was completely wrong. All I said next was, "Feedback is free, and this is my personal interpretation of the situation. I could very well be wrong. All I ask is that you see if maybe 1% of it is true." I did not expect him to do anything with it, but a month later I sat in on another meeting with this team, and to my surprise, he told the team about two actions he had taken. Although he did not share this with them, they were the exact two points that I had given him feedback on.

Later he thanked me, and I told him I admired him for his courage. What he did was take responsibility for his limitations in front of the whole team and this had a powerful, positive effect. When team members acknowledge a mistake and take responsibility, the rest of the team always comes to their aid.

So, feedback works, even if a person is in denial at first. That is why I never allow discussion during the feedback session. The only focus is on giving and receiving it. This is also what balances the introverted and extraverted attitudes in the team. Giving it is an extraverted activity, receiving it an introverted one. After a session, the inner process of each of the participants does the work.

Also, having a discussion would be an extraverted activity and the balance between introversion and extraversion, which is so critical here, would soon be lost. It would consume a lot of time and is more fitting for a process of mediation than feedback. Mediation is usually no longer necessary after a well-structured and facilitated feedback session.

How to Structure Feedback

In structuring feedback, Jung's four functions of consciousness are of great value. Firstly, we can use them to build our own awareness of what we want to give feedback on. Secondly, using all four functions allows the message to have the best chance of being accepted and entering consciousness, of sinking in. And thirdly, it gives the receiver a complete overview of what you have experienced in your consciousness. Let's look at how each of the four functions is used for giving feedback.

Green Sensation - What happened? Give the specific facts and details of a situation. Also, relate the factual impact or effect of an event. Only give facts that are observable and therefore indisputable. The more detail, the better!

Red Feeling - How did this situation make you feel? Did you like it or not? Specify the emotion you felt. Most emotions fall into one of these categories: Mad - Sad - Glad - Afraid.

Yellow Intuition - Why did this situation make you feel this way? How did you interpret the situation? This is your personal narrative or even "drama" that you have attached to the situation. It is what went "through your head" about the situation. Your narrative is always related to the emotion, it is in fact the narrative you have created in your mind that triggers the emotion.

Blue Thinking - What would you like to happen, what would you like to achieve? What would you like the other to continue, improve, stop, or start? With positive feedback, it is usually something like "I want to thank you" and "Please keep doing this." With constructive feedback, it is usually a change in behavior you would like to see.

When giving feedback, it is important to pay attention to your fourth or least preferred function. That element of feedback will be the hardest to formulate. You might tend to dismiss it as unimportant or embarrassing. Or you might confuse this function with another.

Let me give you an example of this. There was a manager who wanted to give his team member some constructive feedback. His dominant function was Blue Thinking, his fourth and least preferred function Red Feeling. In the feedback process, he said with an angry tone, "When you did …, I had the feeling you should never do this again!" As you might have guessed, this did not go over very well. He was confusing Feeling with Thinking. I intervened and asked him to re-formulate his feedback to something like this. "When you did…, I felt angry because … and I want to ask you to not do … but … instead."

The example above also shows how important it is to have a facilitator present who corrects these mistakes and prevents the feedback session from becoming counterproductive. This is especially important for a team inexperienced in this area. A team that has learned this process is able to conduct this on their own, through someone on the team that has developed the skill to facilitate.

The Feedback Process
Ideally, the team sits in a circle with an open space in the middle. Everyone in the team gets feedback forms and is asked to take about 20 minutes to prepare four positive feedback messages and four constructive feedback messages for members of the team.

The first round is about positive feedback. One person starts by getting up, standing in the middle of the circle and inviting someone to give them feedback. Next, the person who received the feedback thanks the feedback giver and invites someone else into the center of the circle to give feedback to. This goes on until everyone has given his or her feedback (4 times). After a short break, this is repeated for constructive feedback.

I do this in an open circle so that everyone can hear all the feedback. This is very important for the "clearing effect" to happen. I am not sure why this is, but this is the input I have received from participants. My own interpretation is that when two people give and receive feedback in front of everyone, it helps the whole team.

Team Effectiveness Scan - You Can Only Manage What You Know

As a team, you need to know what is going well and what isn't. That is where feedback from a Team Effectiveness Scan becomes a valuable tool to use. It helps a team to:
1. Know where it stands

2. Know where it wants to go
3. Use continuous feedback to get there

I have developed a Team Effectiveness Scan that you can take online for free at www.polarityconsulting.com. It is based on questions I developed that give feedback on the functioning of a team in the following areas:
- Direction
- Communication
- Collaboration
- Results

Dutch Orange Team wins Olympic Gold

Two years before the 2012 London Olympics I was asked to facilitate the team development of the Dutch Women's Field Hockey Team by their coach, Max Caldas. It was an unforgettable journey. All the key senior players, as well as the coach, had retired from the team that had won a gold medal at the previous Olympics.

The next generation was in their early twenties, so a new team had to be built with a new coach in less than two years. The odds of repeating a gold medal win with a new team were slim, but the coach and the key players obviously had the "fire in the belly" to go for gold. They knew the meaning of "Individuals play the game, teams win championships." My job was to help them become a stronger unit, but it would have been impossible without the commitment of all the players and especially their captain, Maartje Paumen, and their vice-captain, Naomi van As.

Their coach told me the team had a lot of talent but, whenever there was a major game, they tended to fall apart under pressure. The important question became how to build a strong unity from the diversity of all the individual personalities so that they could handle the pressure. Pressure or stress is not some burden that should be carried and suffered through as if you were a mule: it is a change agent for high performance, for realizing your potential.

Our first session was all about creating awareness on "Why?" the team and the individuals wanted to win a gold medal at the Olympics. A gold medal is a result, and we needed to find a deeper motivation. What we discovered in the following sessions was that this team wanted to change the face of sports, wanted to achieve unity, strength, and renewal every day.

The vice-captain, Naomi van As, wrote in one of her columns, *"Teambuilding is just as important as the physical training. You can have capable people, but that is not enough. We have to be a strong unity that cannot be penetrated from the outside. We did a good job!"*

Within the first few months the team created a purpose statement. The staff and team easily amounted to 30 people, which is a time-consuming and inefficient number of people to work with. So, the statement was created by a group of representatives from the staff and the players in two half-day sessions.

This is what their purpose statement looked like:

Vision

We change sports. We all play on the same team, and yet we are all different. Our strength is the unity in our diversity. We are like a cyclone that grows stronger by the day.

Since it is important to visualize, the team chose an image of a cyclone (Source: NASA).

Mission

Through self-awareness, diversity, and communication we achieve unity, strength, and renewal as a team every day. We help each other every day to play better, both individually and as a team.

Core Values

Support

Definition	We respect and support each other unconditionally.
Behaviors	• Sacrifice yourself for the team • Give your opinion honestly • Show you trust each other • Accept that the other is different

Deliver at the Moment-of-Truth

Definition	Every individual always gives the best of herself, without reservation, without excuses.

Behaviors	<ul><li>Always go to the max, in workouts and games</li><li>Hold others accountable for giving it their best</li><li>Take responsibility and NEVER COMPLAIN, BLAME OTHERS OR MAKE EXCUSES!</li></ul>

Clarity

Definition	We all know what to expect in every situation.
Behaviors	<ul><li>We not only have a plan, we all have the same plan</li><li>We make agreements and hold each other accountable</li><li>We each have a team role from which we act</li></ul>

Motivation

Definition	Every team member knows how to motivate herself and others so that together we radiate passion.
Behaviors	<ul><li>Understand the concerns, needs, and values of every team member</li><li>Use strict and respectful feedback rules</li><li>Stimulate team members in the things they are good at</li></ul>

When a team adopts a purpose statement with awareness and responsibility, the effect is powerful. The whole team starts marching to the same beat. It cuts through the clutter, the static on the line, the unnecessary conflicts and endless debates between individuals. It helps a team find clarity about who they are, what their focus is and how they work together. It is very fulfilling to be a member of such a team.

However… this does not happen overnight.

The purpose statement took about three or four months to create, and the next step was execution. As Nelson Mandela said, *"Vision without action is just a dream, action without vision just passes the time, and vision with action can change the world."*

We did evening sessions once every two months and in between the players and staff had homework assignments and they would e-mail me their results, which I would then use as input for the next session.

The stress simulation games we played were very beneficial. The things that went wrong during these (games) were the same things that went wrong on the pitch. We found ways to deal with these so the team would only become stronger under stress, not weaker. The team also went on a survival retreat with Dutch army officers who helped them bond and become stronger individually, and as a team. This is the role stress should play: as a change agent for higher performance. This team was able to use pressure in this way for which they deserve all the credit.

One of the outcomes of the stress simulation game was that individual players were given specific roles that fitted their personality and drew on their unique strength. Suddenly, less prominent players in the team made important contributions based on their individual qualities. One example: there was a player who was good at analyzing what the problem was whenever the team got "stuck" during a game. Her job was to report it to the captain who acted on it. Slowly but surely a team emerged that could handle the pressure of the semi-finals and finals at the Olympics.

Often, I learn more from my clients than they do from me. The work with this team got me thinking about developing a methodology that helps any team to become high performing. Working with world-class athletes who are put to the test in weekly matches helped uncover what works and what does not.

Celebrating the Dutch hockey team's Olympic Gold Medal in the Netherlands, Captain Maartje Paumen at left, the author at right.

Epilogue

I hope I have been able to demonstrate that polarities are everywhere and that their strength lies in a dynamic balance between the poles whereas their weakness lies in one-sidedness. The challenge is to harness the power of polarities as an individual, team, organization, and even as a nation. My experience is that the power that is unleashed leads to peak performance, authentic impact and a feeling of fulfillment, and happiness.

A critical step in this process is finding the center, the unity that transcends the diversity of your personality. Without this center, transformation cannot take place. It is where the opposite poles of the personality lose their autonomy, their self-centeredness and become connected to the greater whole of your being.

> *There is a complete standstill in a kind of inner center, and the functions do not act automatically anymore. You can bring them out at will, as for instance an airplane can let down the wheels in order to land and then draw them in again when it has to fly. At this stage, the problem of the functions is no longer relevant; the functions have become instruments of a consciousness that is no longer rooted in them or driven by them.*
> (Von Franz, 1998, Chapter 4: The Role of the Inferior Function in Psychic Development)

My invitation to you is to create your own experience of the power of polarities with the help of this book, your personality, the personalities of others and a common center to rotate around.

Appendix I

Symbol of the American Dream: National Mall in Washington, D.C.

America will never be destroyed from the outside. If we falter and lose our freedoms, it will be because we destroyed ourselves.

~ Abraham Lincoln

My dream is of a place and time where America will once again be seen as the last best hope on earth.

~ Abraham Lincoln

The National Mall in Washington, D.C. plays a vital role in the psychological growth and transformation of the American Union of States and, as I will show in this chapter, it is a great example of the Power of Polarities. It is the "Field of Dreams" for the American nation. It is a place of potent symbols, but what do these symbols mean?

For all intents and purposes, I will do a "thought experiment" and treat it as a case of team development for *Team USA.* Very much like the case of the Olympic hockey team I worked with.

Team USA has a remarkable asset, the National Mall. Whenever Team USA is in trouble, the National Mall is the place to turn to and find solutions. As I will show, it is a rich and valuable resource for the transformation of a nation. I have been fortunate to visit it often. When I was younger, my parents took us there, and in my adult life, it has been a place that I have made an effort to visit. And it is high on my bucket list of things to go see with my children.

The National Mall and its monuments are rich with symbolism that reflects the life and memories of the nation. Here is a list of some of the most important ones:
- Franklin Delano Roosevelt Memorial
- Korean War Veterans Memorial
- Thomas Jefferson Memorial
- Vietnam Veterans Memorial
- Martin Luther King, Jr. Memorial
- World War II Memorial
- Washington Monument
- Lincoln Memorial

Let's start in the center, with the Washington Monument. It commemorates George Washington, the "father of the nation," the general who led the US to independence and our first President. He symbolizes the birth and growth of a nation. Interestingly enough, the work on the monument was interrupted by the Civil War, and the upper half of the monument has a different color stone. It symbolizes the scar on a nation that was divided by war. But the Union was saved and the monument completed.

If we superimpose a grid of Jung's four functions of consciousness on the Mall, it looks like this:

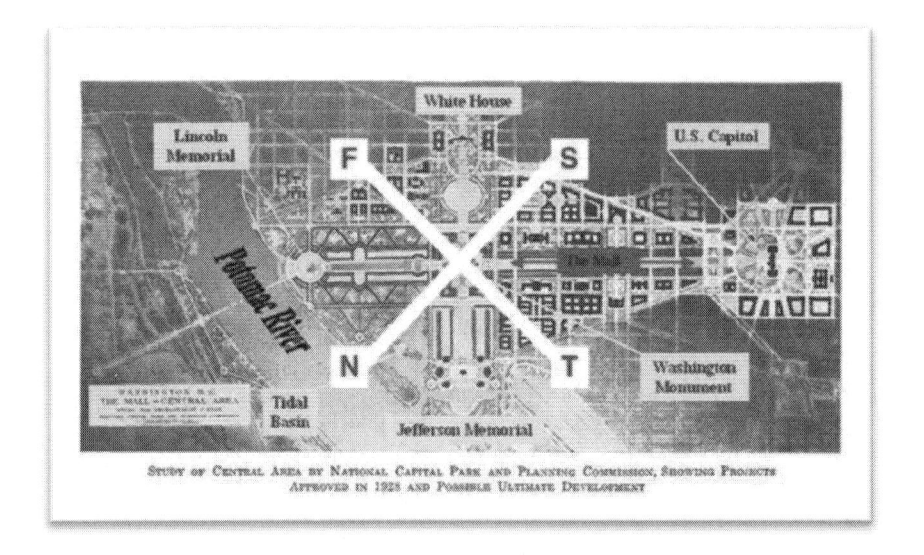

[Figure: Map of the National Mall showing the four quadrants labeled F, S, N, T, with landmarks: Lincoln Memorial, White House, U.S. Capitol, Potomac River, Tidal Basin, Jefferson Memorial, Washington Monument.]

STUDY OF CENTRAL AREA BY NATIONAL CAPITAL PARK AND PLANNING COMMISSION, SHOWING PROJECTS APPROVED IN 1925 AND POSSIBLE ULTIMATE DEVELOPMENT

Each of the four quadrants of the temperaments corresponds to a landmark. Each of them has a critical contribution to make to the nation, which is symbolized by the Washington Monument. It is essential that they work together otherwise the country becomes divided. What is simply remarkable, is that the positions of the landmarks coincide with their typological role.* Allow me to elaborate.

White House: SF - Helper - Terracotta Temperament
The White House is in the quadrant of the Helper with its Green Sensation and Red Feeling qualities. In it is the Oval Office, from where the President runs the country. The role of the president is to help the people he serves, to make sure their needs are met, their problems are solved. This is what people remember about a president. Or in the words of Dale Carnegie:

"Remember that the people you are talking to are a hundred times more interested in themselves and their wants and problems than they are in you and your problems."

The Jungian archetype behind the Helper Temperament is that of the King which points at the fundamental function of the King (or President): to serve the people.

U.S. Capitol: ST - Technician - Teal Temperament

The Technician with his Green Sensation and Blue Thinking functions is good at setting the rules and the standards according to which work will be done. "We do things by the book," the Technician says. This is the job of Congress, to make and pass the laws that represent practical decisions on how the nation is run.

The Jungian archetype behind the Technician Temperament is that of the Warrior which points at the fundamental function of the Warrior (or Congress): set boundaries and protect them.

Jefferson Memorial: NT - Inventor - Turquoise Temperament

The Inventor with his Yellow Intuition and Blue Thinking functions is an independent and free thinker who often has good ideas about how things can be changed and improved. Thomas Jefferson was an inventor, and among his inventions is the polygraph (a copying machine). The Inventor thinks differently and as a result can run into opposition. That is why inside the Memorial you find quotes from Jefferson such as: *"I have sworn upon the altar of God eternal hostility against every form of tyranny over the mind of man."*

The Jungian archetype behind the Inventor Temperament is that of the Magus, which points at the fundamental function of the Magus: to bring change and innovation.

Lincoln Memorial: NF - Visionary - Orange Temperament

The Lincoln Memorial represents the Orange Temperament of the Visionary (NF), who provides a vision of wholeness, harmony, and personal growth. It is said, "Where there is no vision, the people perish." Lincoln's vision for the country saved the United States. He formulated it in his Gettysburg address when he said: *"That this nation under God shall have a new birth of freedom and that government of the people, by the people for the people shall never perish from this earth."*

The Jungian archetype behind the Visionary Temperament is that of the Lover, which points at the fundamental function of the Lover: to hold people together.

The Inferior Function and the Inferior Temperament

As Jung explained the Inferior Function is the function in the personality through which growth and renewal takes place. It is not different for Team USA. Whenever Team USA gets stuck, it needs a "new birth of freedom" which is found in the Red Feeling function and Visionary Temperament. In the case of Team USA this is represented by the Lincoln Memorial, as explained above. For example, it is appropriate and no coincidence that Martin Luther King, Jr. gave his "I Have a Dream" speech in front of the Lincoln Memorial. King presented the nation there with a new vision, a vision where *"people will not be judged by the color of their skin, but by the content of their character."*

We need to look for a moment at the symbolism of the *Reflecting Pool* in front of the Lincoln Memorial. The Memorial and the Pool were designed by the architect Henry Bacon. In 2012 the Pool's water supply was connected to the Tidal Basin whose water comes from the Potomac River. Archetypally water represents the unconscious which psychologically is the source of renewal and growth. From the point of view of the Lincoln Memorial one can see the reflection of the Washington Monument in it. This means there is a symbolic connection with center of the National Mall.

Symbolically this is an enormous resource for Team USA. This is easier to see depending on your personality type (Intuition is function of symbolic consciousness). But think of it, there is a connection to the unconscious (water from the Potomac) and there is the reflection of the center in it, so in a sense the center is being fed by the unconscious (as an Intuitive type myself it is hard to find the right language for this).

What this means symbolically becomes will become clearer when we look at the role of the Washington Monument for the development of Team USA.

Finding the Center for Team USA

Like with any team, these four views all need to come together in the center, the Washington Monument, and they need to serve the central creed of the nation, as formulated by Thomas Jefferson in the Declaration of Independence:

We hold these truths to be self-evident, that all men are created equal, that they are endowed by their Creator with certain unalienable Rights, that among these are Life, Liberty and the pursuit of Happiness. That to secure these rights, Governments are instituted among Men, deriving their just powers from the consent of the governed.

In a very real sense, Jefferson is the Philosopher (NT Temperament) of the nation, and Lincoln the Prophet (NF Temperament). So it makes sense to take into consideration Lincoln's final words of the Gettysburg Address here:

That this nation under God shall have a new birth of freedom and that government of the people, by the people for the people shall never perish from this earth.

If we take these two texts as input, we can start drafting a vision and mission. The vision is a description of the world you want to create. The mission is the central task to realize the vision. With this in mind, a vision and mission statement for Team USA could look something like this:

Vision
To create a society where everyone is treated equally and has a right to live, be free, and pursue that which gives them happiness and fulfillment.

Mission
To ensure equal opportunity and protect the legal rights to life, freedom, and happiness for all citizens through government of the people, by the people, for the people.

The above purpose statement is not complete and needs further concretization. As I have explained in my chapter on the *Power of Purpose*, it needs to be completed with Values and Objectives. But it is a beginning and enough for our thought experiment. If you take a moment to reflect and think of all the problems in Team USA's society and political life, it gives an idea of how all these problems need to be solved to create a society as described above. It sets an aim. The first thing that I notice when I read the vision and mission is that you cannot achieve it when there are over 10 million illegal immigrants who do not have citizenship. That makes it impossible to have government of the people, by the people, for the people. Either they have to be deported, or granted citizenship (or a combination thereof). If I were to facilitate this team, they would find solutions. But since the job of a facilitator is to be neutral, I will refrain from further comments and leave it up to your imagination what these might be.

The Declaration of Independence represents the core of the American nation, for better or for worse. No political party can claim it as their exclusive property. To do so would only create imbalance and weakness. The key to creating this nation and its cyclical rebirths lies in the symbolism of all the different parts of the Mall: The White House, The Capitol, The Jefferson Memorial and the Lincoln Memorial. And you can use it to solve very concrete, practical problems. It is where Intuition with its understanding of symbolism meets Sensation with its understanding of practicalities.

I hope you enjoyed this little "thought experiment" and invite to you have a go at this yourself. Complete this thought experiment with values and objectives using the framework I have laid out in the chapter *The Power of Purpose*. Or apply it to your own team. It is a fun and valuable exercise.

There is one more thing... Life, liberty, and happiness are not exempt from the laws of polarities. Liberty and freedom can only exist if there are limitations and balance. Happiness can only exist if there is awareness of what does and what does not make one truly happy. And finally, as Abraham Lincoln said in his second inauguration speech: "*A house divided against itself cannot stand.*" The four opposing forces of the four typological quadrants must come together and balance their own unique gifts and talents in alignment with a central purpose. Time and time again.

(*) This chapter was inspired by a lecture given by my friend and colleague Dr. Nick Grant, at the Jung Society of Austin in 2013. He is an authority on the MBTI, the famous Jung-based personality instrument. His lecture on the National Mall was based on that instrument. My discussion of this topic is different and based on the concepts in this book.

Appendix II

Other Interpretations of Jung's Psychological Types

The Myers-Briggs Type Indicator® (MBTI®) and the Keirsey Temperament Sorter are two of the most widely used practical applications of Jungian typology. There are some key differences with these two typological systems that are important to note. Every system, every interpretation has its limitations. Also, the one proposed in this book. To more fully realize the potential that Jungian typology offers, it is important to know what these limitations are. But before I discuss these it is important to say something about the enormous positive impact and contribution both systems have made. It far outweighs their limitations.

The true pioneers of the practical application of Jungian typology are Katherine Cook-Briggs and her daughter Isabel Briggs-Myers. In World War II they wanted to help the war effort by finding a way to assist the women who entered the workforce to find the positions they would be most quickly effective at. They created their first set of questions in 1943. Isabel Myers found help in constructing and statistically validating her type indicator from an expert, Edward Hay who at the time was a HR manager at a large bank. One can only admire the love, dedication and expertise with which they created their instrument. Now, almost 75 years later, the Myers-Briggs Type Indicator® (MBTI®) is the most used personality instrument today and has helped millions and millions of people around the world to "recognize and enjoy their gifts". The book *Gifts Differing* Isabel Briggs-Myers published in 1980, is to this date one of the best books on the practical application of Jungian typology. Personally, I like it because it is so pure and original. And the vast number of trainers, coaches and consultants that has applied this instrument, has created a solid body of knowledge on Jungian typology. Carl Jung and society in general owe mother and daughter a great debt in this respect.

How great this gift is, is described so well in the introduction of *Please Understand Me II,* by professor David Keirsey:

> *... Jung's Psychological Types, gathered dust in college libraries, while psychology came to be dominated by Freudian psychodynamics on the one hand, and Pavlovian conditioning on the other...*
> *Breakthroughs in the behavioral sciences often come from outside the field, and Jung's ideas were given new life almost by accident. At mid-century Isabel Myers, a layman, dusted off Jung's Psychological Types and with her mother, Kathryn Briggs, devised a questionnaire for identifying different kinds of personality. She called it "The Myers-Briggs Type Indicator." Largely inspired by Jung's book, the questionnaire was designed to identify sixteen patterns of action and attitude, and it caught on so well that in the 1990s over a million individuals were taking it each year. Interest in personality typology was restored in both America and Europe.*
> (Keirsey, 1984, Ch.1)

Their work also suffers from a limited perspective in some key areas. As does Jung's work. There is a critique of Jung in *Gifts Differing* that I strongly agree with. Isabel Myers critiques Jung in *Gifts Differing* for not spending more time describing the function pairs since that is so important for the practical application of his work. I could not agree more:

Nowhere in Jung's book does he describe these normal, balanced types with an auxiliary process at their disposal. He portrays each process in sharpest focus and with maximum contrast between its extraverted and introverted forms; consequently, he describes the rare, theoretically "pure" types, who have little or no development of the auxiliary. Jung's approach has several unfortunate effects. By ignoring the auxiliary, he bypasses the combinations of perception and judgment and their broad categories of interest in business, people, language, and science.
(Myers, 1980, Ch. 2)

There is one important area where my approach and my interpretation of Jungian typology differs from that in *Gifts Differing*. And the reason I want to address it is not for theoretical purposes, but for practical ones, for making Jung's work more practical and easy to apply to one's life. Just like Isabel Myers does in the quote above.

In their discussion of type dynamics, i.e. how the different functions and attitudes interact, Briggs and Myers believe that if a person has an extraverted preference, then the dominant function is extraverted and the auxiliary function introverted. And vice versa for a person with an introverted preference. Many type practitioners struggle with this interpretation. A friend and former colleague of mine, Paul Scheffer, has written an article on this that is very interesting (APTi Bulletin of Psychological Type, Vol. 33, No. 4, 2010). In it he explains how as an INFP, he (and others) just cannot see his extraverted Intuition. Then he goes on to explain how this interpretation by Briggs and Myers is based on an unfortunate translation error in the English translation of *Psychological Types*. Below I will go a deeper into this issue than he does in his article.

On page 19 of *Gifts Differing* Myers writes about the role of the auxiliary in balancing introversion and extraversion:

The basic principle that the auxiliary provides the needed extraversion for the introverts and needed introversion for the extraverts, is vitally important.
(Myers, 1980, Ch. 2)

Myers continues to explain it is based on the following quote from Jung:

For all the types appearing in practice, the principle holds good that besides the conscious main function there is also a relatively unconscious, auxiliary function which is in every respect different from the nature of the main function.
(Jung, CW 6, § 669)

Which is then interpreted by her as follows:

The operative words are "in every respect." If the auxiliary process differs from the dominant process in every respect, it cannot be introverted where the dominant process is introverted. It has to be extraverted if the dominant process is introverted, and introverted if the dominant process is extraverted.
(Myers, 1980, Ch. 2)

This interpretation would be plausible if the translation had been accurate, but where the English translation says "relatively unconscious," the German original and the Dutch translation are different. They do not read "relatively unconscious" but "relatively conscious." See below the original German text.

Für alle praktisch vorkommenden Typen nun gilt der Grundsatz, daß sie neben der bewußten Hauptfunktion noch eine relativ <u>bewußte</u>, auxiliäre Funktion besitzen, welche in jeder Hinsicht vom Wesen der Hauptfunktion verschieden ist.

The word *"bewußte"* was translated as unconscious, but means conscious. Unconscious would have been *"unbewußte"* in German.

There are a few remarks to be made based on closer scrutiny of this interpretation:
- The subject of the section that this paragraph of Jung is in is called *The Principal and Auxiliary Functions*. The introverted and extraverted attitudes are not mentioned once. So why draw conclusions on the attitudes of these functions?
- The only reason to draw such a conclusion from Jung's writing is if the text had said *unconscious* instead of *conscious*. Because when there is a conscious extraverted preference, the unconscious has to be introverted. But in the original German text that is not the case.
- When Jung writes *"is in every respect different"* he means different and *not* opposite. Like in the following quote from the same section:

Experience shows that the secondary function is always one whose nature is different from, though not antagonistic to, the primary function.
(Jung, CW 6, § 668)

Next in *Gifts Differing*, the Judging/Perceiving scale is introduced. It is used to determine which function is extraverted, the dominant or the auxiliary. An ESTJ, for example, has extraverted Thinking as dominant function and introverted Sensation as auxiliary. An ISTJ, on the other hand, has introverted Sensation as dominant function, and extraverted Thinking as auxiliary. Mother Katherine Briggs created this dimension as follows:

Inclusion of the JP preference in the theory came about as a result of unpublished personality research by Katharine C. Briggs before Jung's Psychological Types was published. The type categories she had devised were entirely consistent with Jung's, but less detailed. Her "meditative type" included all introvert types. Her "spontaneous type" corresponded to the perceptive extraverts, in whom perceptive behavior is at its strongest. Her "executive type" exactly described the extraverted thinkers, and her "sociable type" the extraverted feeling people. When Jung's theory was published in 1923, she saw that it went far beyond her own, and she

made an intensive study of it. Putting together the sentences quoted earlier in this chapter, she interpreted them to mean that the auxiliary process runs the introvert's outer life. She looked at the outer lives of her "meditative" friends to see if this was true and concluded that it was.
(Myers, 1980, Ch. 2)

One can understand how Katherine C. Briggs came to this conclusion. The J/P preference is strictly an extraverted preference in the personality and is used to determine the dominant and auxiliary functions. It was added to Jung's theoretical construct based on a translation error and the resulting misinterpretation of his work. The validation of this with "her meditative friends" is not very convincing, because there can be other explanation for this. The other problem is that since this time there has not been any research that I know of that supports this hypothesis. According to Jung, whether someone has a Perceiving or Judging preference depends on the dominant and inferior function in the personality. If the dominant and inferior functions are Thinking or Feeling, then the personality has a preference for Judging. If the dominant and inferior functions are Sensation or Intuition, the personality has a preference for Perceiving.

I want to stress that for me this does not discredit the MBTI as an instrument. The fourth dimension of the personality (J/P) is a statistically valid one, but the conclusion that in the extraverted personality the auxiliary function is introverted and vice versa, does not seem to be grounded in theory or practice.

I have wondered how, besides the translation error, it was possible that this mistake was made? My explanation is that Katherine C. Briggs (the mother) lived in the early days of Jungian psychology. Jung had barely broken up with Freud and had not even published *Psychological Types* when she was already interested in type and developing her own personality models. She must have been a remarkable woman who was ahead of her time. At the same time, Jungian psychology was not as well developed as it is now. For instance, when Jung uses the conscious-unconscious polarity he really means that the conscious tendency is completely opposite to the unconscious one. In other version, conscious Extraversion constellates Introversion in the unconscious. And vice versa.

Another reason is that Briggs and Meyers wanted to know how a person introverts and extraverts, which is a very important and valid question. In *Gifts Differing* a convincing claim is made that introversion and extraversion have to be balanced.

> *The basic principle that the auxiliary provides the needed extraversion for the introverts and needed introversion for the extraverts is vitally important.*
> (Myers, 1980, Ch. 2)

I both agree and I disagree with the way this process is described in *Gifts Differing*. It is a matter of the right thing in the wrong way. I postulate that functions do not operate in isolation, they are processes that work in triangles (function pairs coupled with an attitude). Which is a claim Briggs also makes, but I do not see her follow through on it. And as I have mentioned before, my experience is that people can both introvert and extravert their dominant function. They can do that because that function is relatively conscious. It is like the front door of a house that you can use both to enter and exit.

If I look at my type, ENFP, the order in which the functions are theoretically used is different if you work from the proposition that the functions act in pairs.

Consciousness	Gifts Differing	Function Pairs
Dominant	Ne	Ne + Fe
2	Fi	Ni + Fi
3	Te	Ne + Te
4	Ni	Ni + Ti
5	Fe	Se + Fe
6	Ti	Si + Fi
7	Se	Se + Te
Inferior	Si	Si + Ti

Note: The first four are relatively conscious, the last four unconscious (i.e. difficult to use consciously). Also note the inferior function pair is Si+Ti and that the inferior function is Sensation.

The consequences of this translation error are pretty huge though. I have been to type conferences in Europe and have met many MBTI practitioners and some tend to hold on to this, well, almost religiously. I understand this, since the point is made so convincingly in *Gifts Differing*, but it has never felt true to me. My inner BS detector never bought it. But that was not enough, I needed to evaluate it using my introverted Thinking function which has resulted in this article.

The reason this approach has been used so successfully is because it is not completely false. Someone like me (ENFP) does have introverted Feeling high in consciousness (as the table above shows). But it is coupled with introverted Intuition (as my dominant function). For my type (ENFP), I interpret the P to mean that the Perceiving function of Intuition is my dominant function, Feeling is auxiliary, Thinking is tertiary and Sensation is my inferior function.

The practical difficulty I see with the way the MBTI has evolved is in recognizing one's own true preferences, especially the recognition of the dominant and inferior function. When one takes the MBTI it is hard to determine. Yes, there is an answer, but is it the right one? For example, I have taken the MBTI together with a close friend of mine. We both come out as ENFP which is gives a fairly good description of both of our personalities. But my friend's dominant function is Feeling and mine is Intuition. My inferior function is Sensation and his is Thinking. This is an important difference in our personalities. And yet we get the same result: Intuition dominant and Sensation inferior. My friend actually has Sensation as tertiary preference. To me this shows the limitation of the J/P scale.

How relevant is this discussion? When we consider that "It is up to each person to recognize his or her true preferences", as Isabel Briggs-Myers said, it is not that relevant. But it does help to take with a grain of salt the biased paradigm of type dynamics that *Gifts Differing* contains, and all the subsequent works that are based on it.

There is another reason that the discussion on type dynamics is not so relevant: personality type does not predict or explain all of human behavior. Based on the situation and based on the conscious or unconscious decisions the ego makes, the order and way in which these functions are used can change. And ultimately that is the goal, to use these functions ethically and morally as the situation requires. That is the great challenge that lasts a life time and much more important.

I am an equally great fan of the late Professor David Keirsey. I found out after his death in 2013 that we both went to Pomona College in California, which is a small liberal arts college, so quite a coincidence. He did important work, especially working for schools as a "corrective interventionist" to help hyperactive children behave themselves and prevent them from being put on Ritalin, which he considered a very destructive drug. I wish I had had the chance to meet him and maybe I did at one of the alumni weekends on campus, but it is unlikely I will ever find out.

His great contribution is the deduction, formulation and illustration of temperaments from the MBTI framework. Temperaments are an important and insightful simplification, as he shows in his work *Please Understand Me II*. About how he came to his four temperaments, he writes:

> *I soon found it convenient and useful to partition Myers's sixteen "types" into four groups, which she herself suggested in saying that all four of what she referred to as the "NFs" were alike in many ways and that all four of the "NTs" were alike in many ways — although what she called the "STs" seemed to me to have very little in common, just as the "SFs" had little in common. However, four earlier contributors, Adickes, Spränger, Kretschmer, and Fromm, each having written of four kinds of personality, helped me to see that Myers's four "SJs" were very much alike, as were her four "SPs." Bingo! People-watching from then on was a lot easier, the four groups being light years apart in their attitudes and actions.*
> (Keirsey, 1984, Ch. 2)

My critique here is that he did not base his temperaments on Jung, but on other writers. They were leading, not Jung. I do not find anywhere that he compared their writing with Jung's. This is a real pity because Jung used the first 9 chapters of *Psychological Types* to evaluate the "Type Problems" in other schools of thought. Jung actually discusses the work of Plato, Aristotle, Claudius Galen and Ernst Kretschmer. I can only assume that Keirsey did not study these chapters. The questions is, would he have reached a different conclusion if he had? I would think so, but unfortunately we will never find out since he passed away in 2013.

Also, the descriptions by Isabel Myers which were based on the addition of her mother's J/P construct which I have commented on above. I believe it was for Keirsey a practical and convenient way to use the MBTI framework to identify his temperaments. It adds an unnecessary and incorrect complication. It draws away attention from what Jungian analyst and author of *Energies and Patterns in Psychological Type,* John Beebe calls the *backbone* of the personality, the interplay between the dominant and inferior function (which cannot be clearly ascertained using the J/P construct). John Beebe writes:

When there is development of both the superior and the inferior functions, we can speak of a 'spine' of consciousness that gives a personality backbone.
(Beebe, 2017, Ch. 8)

I hope I have done enough justice to the work of Isabel Myers and David Keirsey, for their contributions have been huge. As Keirsey writes, without Katherine Cook-Briggs and Isabel Briggs-Myers, Jungian typology might be in the archives of humanity.

There is a lot more I could say about this subject, but if I do this book will never get finished. I am looking forward to a fruitful dialogue with students of type on this subject.

Appendix III

1995 Interview with Robert A. Johnson

Robert A. Johnson is a renowned Jungian analyst, author, and lecturer. His books have sold more than 3 million copies. He was born in Portland, Oregon in 1921 and studied at the University of Oregon and Stanford University. When he was 24, he studied with Krishnamurti, and when he was 26, he went to Zürich in Switzerland to study at the C.G. Jung Institute. There he met Carl and Emma Jung and went into analysis with Jolande Jacobi.

In 1974, he lectured at St. Paul's Cathedral in San Diego where he worked with John A. Sanford, an Episcopal priest who had his lectures transcribed and published as *He: Understanding Masculine Psychology*. The book soon became a bestseller and was followed by *She*, *We*, *Inner Work*, *Ecstasy*, *Transformation*, *Femininity Lost and Regained*, *Owning Your Own Shadow*, *The Fisher King and the Handless Maiden*, *Balancing Heaven and Earth*, *Contentment*, *Living Your Unlived Life* and *Inner Gold*.

In 2002 he received an honorary doctorate from Pacifica Graduate Institute in California. He currently lives in a nursing home in San Diego, California.

The interview was conducted on March 29, 1995, at the home of Robert in Encinitas, California. It was originally intended to be published in a Dutch magazine but for various reasons that did not work out and it finds its debut here.

Can you tell us about your life?

I was born in 1921 in Portland Oregon from a Swedish father and a Canadian mother. It was a very bad marriage. My early days were very difficult. Finally, I was "parked" with my grandmother, and she raised me. That has had a curious effect on me. I have a grandmother complex, where most people have a mother complex.

In my late teens and all through my twenties life was just hellish, it was a nightmare. I only barely survived. Part of the reason was that I was so wounded by my childhood. And I forgot to tell you. I was very badly injured in an automobile accident when I was 11, and I lost a leg. That terminated my childhood and made adolescence a very difficult time. I buried myself in music. I lived in music from age 16 until age 30 and prepared a musical career. Finally, my life became so painful and so near impossible that a friend of mine simply ordered me to go see a Jungian analyst. And I did. This was Fritz Künkel in San Francisco. He saved my life. He taught me a language which was coherent and which opened up the inner world to me. And this was a world that was possible for me because it was coherent.

By incredibly good fortune I met Carl Jung. I call it a series of slender threads. If I would ever write an autobiography - which I do not intend to - I would call it Slender Threads because all of the important things that have happened to me have hung together by these slenderest of threads. I happened to be somewhere, and I happened to have a conversation with somebody. And by a number of these slender threads, I ended up in Carl Jung's study in Zürich and had found not only a cure but also a profession.

You met Carl Jung in person. Could you say something about your first encounter with him?

It was a dramatic thing. Talk about slender threads; it was one of the slenderest. I hardly got there. It took all the combined forces of heaven to set that meeting. I could never have managed it out of my own intelligence.

I was in Zürich, which was another slender thread, preceded by another slender thread. And I was doing analysis with Jolande Jacobi, who was one of Jung's close followers. She was probably the most unsuitable analyst for me where her temperament was concerned. She had extraverted thinking where I have introverted feeling. She conducted her analytical hours pacing the floor. She was a bundle of energy and very domineering. One day I had a huge, big dream. In retrospect, I think I can see why it frightened her. She evaded it. She said, "That's an old man's dream. You shouldn't dream dreams like that. We are not going to talk about it."

This wasn't satisfactory to me. I had had the dream whether I should or not. And it's true, I was 26 years, and it was too heavy a weight to put on a 26-year-old. So, I walked out on her, for which she never forgave me. I went to Mrs. Jung and asked for an hour with her. Mrs. Jung was highly introverted, a very quiet, graceful, and courteous person. So, I told her the dream. She did not know what to do with it. But she honored it and listened to it. She told the dream to Dr. Jung that night, and he told her he wanted to talk to me. In about 3 hours he told me who I was, what I should do, what I should not do, what to trust, what not to trust. It was an extraordinary experience. He told me to stay with myself, not to marry, not to join anything. He encouraged me a great deal. He said, "The collective unconscious will support you." Which it has. I've worried myself sick, but it has always come through. These slender threads have never failed me. But I didn't know that. I didn't have faith in that.

How did he know what was right for you?

He only knew the dream. And yet he knew so much about me. He had a rare ability which he was famous for. People would come in and start asking him something. Then suddenly, he would cut them off, in the middle of a sentence - he was a rude man too - and would start talking about something else. Just off he would go. And invariably - if they would listen - it was what they ought to hear, not what they wanted to hear. He had a kind of clairvoyance. It must have been extremely painful for him to endure. He knew too much. That was his burden. It must have been torture.

I am interested now and preoccupied with the Moses complex. You know the story of Moses in the Old Testament? He led the people to the promised land but did not enter the promised land himself. He stayed behind while Joshua led the people into the promised land. It is more complicated than that, but I am watching so many great people, great leaders, who lead miserable personal lives. I call this the Moses complex. They lead people to the promised land but are not allowed into it themselves. Jung was the first one I encountered who suffered from this.

But I am not doing that. I am doing better for some reason. Partly because I ceased doing practically everything in the outer world so that I store all my energy for the inner world. I count myself a happy person.

But doesn't the inner world demand you to do things in the outer world?

Well, sometimes people call me to do interviews, as you did. And I do one conference a month. And I have done my books. That is enough.

So, you became an analyst because Jung told you to, is that correct?

Yes. And the strange thing is that all of this is not an adequate reason for the Jungian society to call me a Jungian analyst, they don't recognize me because I did not go through their school, through their program. And yet I was analyzed by six different analysts each teaching me about a different facet of myself.

I had a wonderful time in 1954. I took four months and went to London to study with Dr. Toni Sussman, who was a student of Jung's and authorized by Jung to train analysts. I had four months with her, an hour every day. I had a superb training with her. She was a wonderful person. She was then just about my present age which is awesome for me to think of because I was in my early 30's. She was 4'11" tall; her father was a Hasidic Spanish Jew, her mother a Swedish gentile and she was an ardent, almost belligerent Roman Catholic. We got on tremendously well. A wonderful teaching, training, master/student relationship. Some of my best training happened there.

So, all this time you were training to be an analyst, but outside of an official program of one of the institutes? And that is why you are not recognized?

Jung told me to get out of the institute in Zürich. He said, "This is not the way to train analysts." The old way of master and student is the correct way. The institute in Zürich has just split into two warring factions. The Jungian movement is doing exactly what Christianity did, except faster. Very painful.

Loneliness has been the worst suffering of my life. Early in my life, I wanted to belong somewhere. I wanted to be a junior member of some community somewhere. They wouldn't let me. But that was correct. I know it to be correct.

Why? What would that have taken away from you?

I would have been a collective creature then. I would have been a tribal member, so to speak, which is what I wanted for so long. Any youth hungers for that. It wouldn't have been correct. Jung knew that and when he gave me his instructions he told me "Don't you ever join anything." Of course, I went out and joined anything I could get my hands on because I was so lonely, but none of them ever worked.

Loneliness is a big problem for a lot of people. What could you say to people suffering from loneliness?

Sometimes one must have courage enough and intelligence enough to rise out of one's loneliness and do something about it. Go and marry, go ahead and have your family. Establish your profession, get a circle of friends, buy a house. Settle yourself. Or, for somebody else, as Jung advised me, "Look, forget about all of that. You are going to sit in your solitude." It depends on who you are.

Most people do not look at loneliness as a good thing. What good is there in loneliness?

It is awful. It is the worst kind of torture. When Dante was describing the ten layers of hell, the bottom one, the worst one is frozen. This is the place of loneliness. It is frozen. It is immobile, dead, nothing moves. That is the worst torture of all. Some of the other layers are full of flames, and that's better.

Loneliness is a pathology and a destructive experience. Aloneness, on the other hand, is close to enlightenment. Very gradually my loneliness transforms into aloneness. I read a statement of one of the medieval mystics to that effect. He wrote, "the only cure for loneliness is aloneness." I knew I was hearing the right medicine. At first, someone may hear this and think, "That's true," but he cannot do it. That's a chore for a lifetime. There is a candid Buddhist saying: "All suffering is a too close proximity of God which one cannot stand." This applies to loneliness also.

For Carl Jung individuation was a central concept. What is individuation and why is it so important?

Individuation is the meaning of life. It is what one is born on the face of the earth to do. In the western world, there is a word which touches this: vocation, or that which one is called to do. I like the poetic image of being called. Socrates thought he had a daemon, not a demon but a daemon, sitting on his left shoulder, who advised him, or reprimanded him. That was in a way the calling of Socrates.

One is tall or short, blue eyed or brown eyed, introverted or extraverted; all of one's being at birth is the equipment for accomplishing what one is on the face of the earth to do. One is a doctor, or a poet, or a healer, or an artist. One is destined to have children or destined to be solitary. All of these things are inborn. There is a Hindu term for this called dharma. One arrives on the earth with one's dharma, that which one is ordained to do or ordained to be. And Jung's name for this is individuation. He would be the very first to say that he is only talking about a very old concept. In fact, he said he prepared nothing new in his life. He was talking about things that had been the heritage of humankind since the earliest times. He was only presenting it afresh. And it is important; there is nothing more important. If individuation is that which one is set on the face of the earth to accomplish, then to find one's dharma or vocation or individuation is the one criteria of success on the face of the earth.

Can countries or cultures or nations individuate? What is their role in the individuation process?

Yes, you caught me in my extreme introversion. I talk about these things in their smallest unit, the individual. Of course, nations and cultures have this too, and they too have to find their dharma. This all implies that there is an intelligence or - I shy away from the word god, but there is no real alternative for it - that is running all of these things. Italians were made to be Italians, the Swedes to be Swedes and you are you. That is the miracle of this afternoon, you are you.

When I met Jung, he told me to be true to myself, and true to my type. And that is what I wish for you. If you go against your typological makeup, you go against your grain, and you will get splinters. Go with it, and your life will have ease, flow, and purpose.

In your books, you use old stories or myths like the myth of Parsifal and the myth of Tristan and Isolde. Why do you use myths? What is a myth?

Myths are the language of the unconscious in a collective form. And dreams are the language of the unconscious in a personal form. It is how the unconscious communicates with us, and it uses symbolic language, not literal language. So mythology is the dream of a culture. And if one can understand the dream of a culture one can understand the workings of the nature of god in that culture. Myths and dreams both are the speech of god.

The myths you use are hundreds of years old. Why is it that myths still have meaning after hundreds or thousands of years?

The genetic structure of the human body of 2000 years ago would be highly relevant right now. It doesn't change. The form of it changes. Some of the old myths are particularly direct, simple, and easily assimilable for that reason. There are modern myths too. The difficulty with a contemporary myth is that we are so close to it that it is hard to get a perspective on it. The mythology of the 12th century is particularly interesting to me because so many of the things we are enjoying and struggling with now were being formulated at a mythological level then. If we can understand the two or three great myths that erupted in western Europe in the 12th century, we can get a very good diagram of who we are now, of what we're struggling with, and the tools we have and the dangers that we face. Every man struggles with the myth of Tristan and Isolde.

But the fact that we struggle with it means that we have not finished it, that it is an issue we are still trying to deal with?

That's right. Tristan and Isolde is about male/female relationships. Parsifal is about the young masculine hero. Tristan and Isolde is the one unfinished myth in Western mythology. And that makes me very pessimistic. Even in the myth Tristan and Isolde, I found no answer to their situation or dilemma except death. It is the hardest of all myths to assimilate now. Parsifal, his journeys, his struggles and his knighthood, that all came out well. Parsifal found his grail castle. But Tristan and Isolde is still unfinished business.

Does that mean we are doing well on the level of the conquering hero, but not well in the area of relationships?

Yes. These are prototypes. These are diagrams of our psyche. And you can see in society that we build much better concords and airbuses than we build marriages. This is unfinished business in the western psyche.

Is this myth unfolding in a positive or negative way?

It is largely going negative. More than 50% of the American marriages end up in a divorce. Marriage as an institution is not workable at present. And I don't know any alternative. On Monday, Wednesday, and Friday I am optimistic that this is an evolutionary stage that we have to go through and painfully we will come out with something better. And Tuesday, Thursday, and Saturday I am not very optimistic.

What do you think Western man can do to take this myth further?

The myth itself is highly instructive and gives at least the first step of one's enlightenment, but the western world absolutely refuses to look at this information. The first step is to differentiate between loving somebody and being in love with somebody. Fortunately, we have that distinction in our language. The western world believes that marriage should be based on falling in love. And yet, that is an extremely poor basis for marriage. Falling in love is a religious experience. One has seen the goddess or the god in one's companion. And one cannot marry a god or goddess. Nobody can. But the faculty of love, the faculty of appreciating somebody and bending one's life to accord to that person is a human faculty. Marriage can be based on that. But "falling in love" which Hollywood keeps perpetuating is not a good basis and yet we persist in that idea.

Apparently, we all dream, although we are not always aware of it. Most people remember a dream sometimes. When people remember a dream, what should they do with it?

I believe that everybody dreams all the time, 24 hours a day. It is as if there is a cinema screen in the back of your mind on which a drama takes place all the time. The dream goes on all the time, day and night. But one catches the dream more easily at night because one is quiet enough. But it is possible to catch your dream in the daytime. That is what we call the art of active imagination. If you - so to speak - pull down the blinds in your consciousness and darken things a little bit, and be quiet enough, you will see the dream going on. You can also take part in the dream which is a very powerful thing to do. My religious life lives itself out almost entirely in that art. It is my idea of a religious experience: to take part in a dream.

You ask me what to do when you have a dream. For the most part, not always, dreams are subjective. They are a portrayal what goes on inside of you as if the master playwright wanted to give you some information exclusively about you. And so this master playwright made a play and staged it to portray to you what is going on in the multiple personalities that make up you. The good guy, the bad guy, the heroine, the dragons, the miracles and on and on. They are first of all the portrayal of the drama that is going on exclusively inside of yourself.

But everybody wants to jump outside with their dreams. It is tendency most people have. If, say, tonight you dream of me, the most intelligent way to go about the dream, and the first thing to try is to inquire about the Robert Johnson inside of you. Don't try to put it on me. It is a high discipline to take responsibility for your own dream.

Now sometimes dreams are objective. You must know, though, that I do not think the inside and the outside are different. In fact, I think we are in error to divide inside and outside, but we do. I do not think inside and outside are different, but our consciousness is based on that assumption. So it is best to start inside with your dream.

You say inside and outside are not different?

I have good reason to think that they are not different.

But what do you mean when you say they are not different? The outside you can touch, it is tangible. The inside I cannot touch.

Tonight, I will touch you in your dream. I have an analogy which does not mean much to a lot of people, though it thrills me. Suppose someone was beating a gong sitting out there. And my eyes would register the motion. I would say he raises his hand and the mallet touches the drumhead, and it bounces off. That is what my eyes say. Now my ears say something quite different. I hear this sound. If these two events were separate, I would be utterly naive about the experience, and I would say: "You sense this, but I sense that." And it would not dawn on me that I am witnessing the same event through different faculties. To carry that analogy on, I think for me to watch you this afternoon with my conscious faculties and perhaps to dream about you tonight are two ways to report the same event. They are not different. But they seem different and disconnected. But that is a mistake.

Short of enlightenment one does not feel that way, one does not function that way, one does not experience the inside and the outside as the same. So therefore, with a dream, it is best to start with taking it inwardly.

What are the practical steps you must go through in dream work?

Well, for this you have to read my book "Inner Work." There are four stages. First, you identify the elements of the dream and write down your associations with them. What does each element mean to you personally? Perhaps you dream of a friend, what is that friend like? Next, find the dynamics of these elements in your daily life. What concrete attitudes, events, moods, emotions, etc. are these elements symbols of? If you dream of an angry person, where are you angry? The third step is the interpretation, the message of the dream. It is important to remember that every detail has a message and matters. Needless to say, this is a lot of work, hence the title "Inner Work."

Could you say something about your first series of books He, She and We. You did not write them until later in your life. Why?

The book *He* probably is one of the strangest books in publishing history that I know of. I did four lectures for a priest friend of mine in St. Paul Church in San Diego. And unbeknownst to me he recorded the four lectures and got the church secretary to transcribe them, tidy them up, send them to a little publisher. They accepted and then he told me what he had done. So, I never wrote the book.

All my books come from lectures. I have the kind of mentality - characteristic of introverted feeling people - that unless I have another pair of eyes to look at, my intelligence doesn't function. I can't think. So it is when I am in relatedness that I can think. You are drawing the best out of me today because you are a human being and we have a good report, so my intelligence rises. But I wasn't ready to write these books earlier. I am very much dominated by the archetype of the puer aeternus, I am the kind of person that develops slowly.

Do you know anything about Holland?

I am a great lover of Vermeer. I have a copy of The Music Lesson. It pictures the very ideal of serenity and beauty and dignity. I think the most important thing that happened to me in the last ten years or so and elicited in my book *Owning Your Own Shadow* is a concept that as humans we have two duties or faculties. One is the religious faculty which is to pull everything together, to pull together the dark and the light. And there is the cultural faculty which is to take things apart and keep the good. And Vermeer makes such a beautiful cultural statement. Because everything is in order, things are so beautiful, so clean, so precise. The light is clear. It is the very epitome of order. And I love that.

The torture of mankind, and it grows worse as man gains greater capacity of differentiation, is that the laws pertaining to these two faculties are diametrically opposed to each other. This is the suffering of mankind. Jung said that this is the crucifixion we all must suffer from.

Almost any pair of opposites which you might bring up is included in this. It is simply the crucifixion of any sensible man that he has to be in service of both of these faculties. Mostly one serves the cultural faculty early in life. You are busy with your marriage and your education and your profession, gaining enough money, finding your place. These are all cultural values. You are struggling for the good. The latter half of one's life is a struggle to put these all back together again. To find some coherent meaning for these things. The best way to get through one's crucifixion is to take it straight. If you evade it, then you can get into symptoms of depressions and anxieties.

How are you doing in this respect?

The early part of my life did not go very well because I had such a profound religious experience early in my life. It nearly knocked the cultural capacity out of me. Nobody could convince me that the cultural was important. It was as if I had been blinded by a vision of something else. But the second half of my life has been better than I ever could have imagined or hoped it could be.

Posing for a photo with Robert Johnson in his backyard. Which of the two is more introverted and which more extraverted?

Bibliography

Beebe, John. *Energies and Patterns in Psychological Type*: *The Reservoir of Consciousness*. Digital edition Kindle: Routledge, Taylor & Francis Group, 2017 (1st ed. Routledge, 2016)

Cain, Susan. *Quiet: The Power of Introverts in a World That Can't Stop Talking.* Digital edition Kindle: Random House, Broadway Books, 2012.

Chang, J., M. Patria and L. Effron. "Sebastian Junger's 'Last Patrol' Closes His Chapter on War, Looks at Life Outside Combat." ABC News website, 2014. Link: http://abcnews.go.com/Entertainment/sebastian-jungers-patrol-closes-chapter-war-life-combat/story?id=26710740 (Accessed 23 August 2017)

Covey, Stephen. *The 7 Habits of Highly Effective People*: *Powerful Lessons in Personal Change*. Digital edition Kindle: Rosetta Books, 2013 (1st ed. New York, NY: Free Press, 1988)

Fiddis, Richard. "The Importance of STEM Education to the Economy," *CEO Magazine*, 12 June 2017. Link: http://www.theceomagazine.com/business/importance-stem-education-economy/ (Accessed 23 August 2017)

Frankl, Victor. *Man's Search for Meaning*: *An Introduction to Logotherapy*. Touchstone, 1984 (3rd ed.) (1st German ed. Vienna: Verlag fur Jugend und Volk, 1946; 1st English edition: Boston, MA: Beacon Press, 1959)

Franz, Marie-Louise von, and James Hillman. *Lectures on Jung's Typology*. 1998. Digital edition Kindle: Woodstock, CT: Spring Publications, 2013 (1st ed. Woodstock, CT: Spring Publications, 1986)

Gaiman, Neil. The Sandman, Vol. 9: The Kindly Ones. Digital edition Kindle: Vertigo; Gph edition, 2011 (1st ed. DC Comics, 1996)

Giannini, John L. *Compass of the Soul*: *Archetypal Guides to a Fuller Life*. Gainesville, FL: Center for Applications of Psychological Type, 2004. Print

Jacobi, Jolande. *The Psychology of C.G. Jung*. New Haven, CT: Yale UP, 1973. Print

Johnson, Robert A., and Jerry M. Ruhl. *Balancing Heaven and Earth*: *A Memoir of Visions, Dreams, and Realizations*. Digital edition Kindle: HarperCollins e-books, 2009 (1st ed. Shaftesbury: Element Books, 2000)

Johnson, Robert A. *Owning Your Own Shadow*: *Understanding the Dark Side of the Psyche*. San Francisco, CA: HarperSanFrancisco, 1993. Print

Jung, C. G. *Memories, Dreams, Reflections*. Trans. Richard Winston and Clara Winston. Ed. Aniela Jaffe. Digital edition Kindle: Vintage; Reissue edition, 1989 (1st ed. New York, NY: Vintage Books, 1961)

Jung, C.G., and Hans Schmid-Guisan. *The Question of Psychological Types*: *The Correspondence of C. G. Jung and Hans Schmid-Guisan, 1915-1916*. Comp. John Beebe. Princeton, NJ: Princeton University Press, 2013. Print

Jung, C.G. *The Collected Works of C.G. Jung*: *Complete Digital Edition*. Eds. Adler, G., Fordham, M., Read, H. Digital edition Princeton, NJ: Princeton University: The Trustees of Princeton University, 2014

The designation CW in the book refers to the 20 volumes of Jung's Collected Works:

    CW 1: Volume 1 – Psychiatric Studies (1970)
    CW 2: Volume II – Experimental Researches (1973)
    CW 3: Volume III – Psychogenesis of Mental Disease (1960)
    CW 4: Volume IV – Freud & Psychoanalysis (1961)

CW 5: Volume V – Symbols of Transformation (1967, a revision of Psychology of the Unconscious, 1912)
CW 6: Volume VI – Psychological Types (1971)
CW 7: Volume VII – Two Essays on Analytical Psychology (1967)
CW 8I: Volume VIII – Structure & Dynamics of the Psyche (1969)
CW 9i: Volume IX (Part 1) – Archetypes and the Collective Unconscious (1969)
CW 9ii: Volume (Part 2) – Aion: Researches into the Phenomenology of the Self (1969)
CW 10: Volume X – Civilization in Transition (1970)
CW 11: Volume XI – Psychology and Religion: West and East (1970)
CW 12: Volume XII – Psychology and Alchemy (1968)
CW 13: Volume XIII – Alchemical Studies (1968)
CW 14: Volume XIV – Mysterium Coniunctionis (1970)
CW 15: Volume XV – Spirit in Man, Art, and Literature (1966)
CW 16: Volume XVI – Practice of Psychotherapy (1966)
CW 17: Volume XVII – Development of Personality (1954)
CW 18: Volume XVIII – The Symbolic Life (1977)
CW 19: Volume XIX – General Bibliography (Revised Edition) (1990)
CW 20: Volume XX – General Index (1979)

Jung, C.G. *Modern Psychology: ETH Lectures, Volume 4. Psychological Typology, Winter semester 1935/36 and Summer semester 1936*. Trans. E. Falzeder, M. Kyburz and J. Peck. Eds. E. Falzeder and M. Liebscher. Accepted for publication by Princeton University Press.

Kushner, Harold. *When Bad Things Happen to Good People*. Digital edition Kindle: Anchor; Anv edition, 2007 (1st ed. New York, NY: Random House Inc., 1981)

Keirsey, David. *Please Understand Me II*. Digital edition Kindle: Prometheus, 1998.

Marlantes, Karl. *What It Is Like to Go to War*. New York, NY: Grove Press, 2012. Digital edition Kindle: Atlantic Monthly Press; Reprint edition, 2011 (1st ed. Atlantic Monthly Press, 2011)

Martin, P. W. *Experiment in Depth: A Study of the Work of Jung, Eliot and Toynbee*. London: Routledge, 1955. Print

William McGuire & R.F.C. Hull, eds. *C.G. Jung Speaking, Interviews and Encounters*, Princeton, NJ: Princeton University Press, 1987. Print

William McGuire & Sonu Shamdasani, eds. *Notes of the Seminar on Analytical Psychology given in 1925 by C.G. Jung, 1989 and 2012*. Princeton, NJ: Princeton University Press, 2012. Print

Moore, Robert L., and Douglas Gillette. *King, Warrior, Magician, Lover*: *Rediscovering the Archetypes of the Mature Masculine*. Digital edition Kindle: HarperOne; Reprint edition, 2013 (1st ed. San Francisco, CA: HarperSanFrancisco, 1991)

Myers, Isabel Briggs, and Peter B. Myers. *Gifts Differing*: *Understanding Personality Type*. Digital edition Kindle: Palo Alto, CA: Davies-Black Pub, 2002 (1st ed. Davies-Black Publishing, United States, 1980)

Odom, Jesse. *Through Our Eyes*: *Live, Die, Cry, Kill, Fear, Hope, and Cope*. Rock Hill, SC: Bella Rosa Books, 2008. Print

Stein, Murray. *Jung's Map of the Soul*: *An Introduction*. Chicago, Ill.: Open Court, 2006, n.p. Print

Stein, Murray. *The Principle of Individuation*: *Toward the Development of Human Consciousness*. Wilmette, Ill: Chiron Publications, 2006. Print

Suzuki, D. T. *Essays in Zen Buddhism*, First Series, London/New York, Published for the Buddhist Society, London: Rider, 1926. Print

Vernon, Mark. Philosophy and Life Blog, 2011. Link: https://www.markvernon.com/blog

Weissberg, Roger P. et al., The Impact of Enhancing Student's Social and Emotional Learning: A Meta-Analysis of School Based Universal Interventions, Child Development, January 2011 (Volume 82, Number 1, Pages 405-432).

Wheelwright, Joseph B. *Psychological Types*. San Francisco: C.G. Jung Institute of San Francisco, CA, 1973. Print

Wheelwright, Joseph B. *St. George and the Dandelion: 40 Years of Practice as a Jungian Analyst*. Ed. Audrey Hilliard. Blodgett. San Francisco, CA: C.G. Jung Institute of San Francisco, 1982. Print

Wilde, Douglas. Teamology: The Construction and Organization of Effective Teams.
Digital edition Kindle: Springer London, 2008

Disclaimer

Psychology and typology are social sciences and differ from natural sciences in the sense that they are more descriptive and experimental and less rigorous because of the limited possibilities to engage in double-blind, controlled experiments.

Assessing your personality is not akin to taking your temperature. For instance, completing a questionnaire is a subjective experience, and no conclusions should be made without careful reflection. The real value of a typology questionnaire is that it offers an opportunity for self-reflection. It usually takes several iterations of a personality questionnaire before one finds one's "true type."

The greatest disclaimer to Jung's theory of the personality has perhaps been made by Jung himself:

> *... every individual is an exception to the rule. Hence one can never give a description of a type, no matter how complete, that would apply to more than one individual, despite the fact that in some ways it aptly characterizes thousands of others. Conformity is one side of a man, uniqueness is the other.*
> (Jung, CW 6, § 895)

The content of this book is based on rigorous reflection on 30 years of experience with Jungian psychology and typology. It is intended to be neither scientific nor complete. Every year of additional experience will undoubtedly lead to new insights which hopefully will be integrated into a revised edition sometime in the future.

I too suffer from the affliction that Jung described as "the insight that every judgment made by an individual is conditioned by his personality type and that every point of view is necessarily relative." (*Memories, Dreams and Reflections*, p. 207). Mine is that of an extraverted intuitive type with feeling as auxiliary function, as I am sure is reflected in this book.

There is a lot more to say about this life-changing subject than I could fit in this book. Hopefully, it will add a drop to the vast ocean of knowledge that is out there already.

I believe this book can be valuable to those wanting to examine their life, whether as an individual, a team, or an organization. I hope this book will help you experience the power of polarities in your own individual way so that you can have a positive and unique impact on the world in which you live.

Acknowledgements

I would like to thank all the clients I have been privileged to work with. It has been an honor to serve you and help you achieve your goals. My commitment to you is to pass everything I have learned from you on to others.

Many people have shown me the way by shedding light on my path, mentoring me and encouraging me to go forward. Amongst them are Prof. Fred Sontag, Prof. Alma Zook, Dr. Betty van Baaren, Prof. Wim Driehuis, Dr. Geert Reuten, Prof. Jaap van Duijn, Prof. Henk Jager, Prof. Arnold Heertje, Pauline Botden, Mauk Pieper, Robert A. Johnson, Robert Moore, Michael Meade, Robert Stamboliev, Willem Poppeliers, Lydia Kimman, Marijke Schneider-Blomjous, Siegmar Gerken, Hans Boudens, Pieter Stenfert, Andi Lothian, Hans-Paul Sparenberg, Anne Buchanan, Johan Kos, Peter Zonneveld, Carla Stolk, Max Caldas, Johan and Joke Leeuw, Dr. Nick Grant, Russell Forsyth, Dr. Priscilla Murr, Dr. Murray Stein, Pittman McGehee D.D., Rob Foree, Phil Haag, Beth McGrath, Craig Stevens and Nick Covelli. Thank you for touching my life and for your indispensable support and guidance.

A special thanks and acknowledgement to all my friends and former colleagues at Insights Learning and Development. From you I learned so much, especially what it means "to live, love, learn and leave a legacy." I miss you and wish you the best.

I also want to express my gratitude to the people who have helped edit this book. Amongst them are Victoria Darling, my parents Anne and Hans van der Steur, my brother Pieter and sister Mary van der Steur, as well as Mark Poysden and Stef Osadzinski. For the publishing process, I had a great collaboration with Jyotsna and Sushmitha at www.happyselfpublishing.com.

Last and most, I want to honor and thank all the generations that came before me. Specifically, I want to thank all my ancestors who gave me life that I can express and pass on to next generations. Jung always emphasized it is important we know our history and our origin so that we may better know who we are. So here we go. My great grandparents: Jim Gregory & Ruth Miller, Adrianus van der Steur & Elizabeth Pander, Melvin Kuhns & Emma Vogelgesang, Nicolaas van der Sleen & Aaltje Mandemaker. My grandparents: Piet van der Steur & Marietje van der Sleen, Dwight Kuhns & Mattie Gregory. And my parents: Hans van der Steur & Anne Kuhns. Thank you and all those that came before you for taking on the role and responsibility of parents, creating new life and channeling love into this world.

About the Author

John van der Steur grew up in the Netherlands. He attended Pomona College in California as a Fulbright Scholar. He has a graduate degree in Economics from the University of Amsterdam.

After his studies, John joined Accenture and served clients in the Netherlands, the UK, Belgium and Germany. He then worked for Nolan, Norton & Co., the strategic management group of KPMG in the Netherlands. In 2002, he founded Insights Learning & Development in the Benelux where he serviced global clients in Europe, Asia and Africa. After moving to Austin, Texas, he left Insights Benelux and founded Polarity Consulting, LLC.

He has worked with thousands of individuals and hundreds of teams to help them achieve their goals. Clients include corporate teams and Olympic gold medalists. John is also a member of the Association of Psychological Type International.

In his own words:

"I have had a lifelong fascination with the psychology of Carl Jung and have specialized myself in the practical application of his work. I have experienced how it can change outcomes and even change lives. I am passionate about helping people discover their personalities and see what unique capabilities they bring to the table. This book is the result of 30 years of experience in this field.

I believe you must know yourself if you want to navigate and thrive in today's chaotic world. Understand your personality, your mind, your heart. And most importantly, your unique purpose or calling in this world.

I am the product of a Dutch father and an American mother and was raised in the Netherlands. Currently, I live in Austin and am the proud father of two tall Dutch-American girls age nine and eleven."

Contact Information:

E : john@polarityconsulting.com
M : +1 (512) 739-8482
W : www.polarityconsulting.com

Printed in Great
Britain
by Amazon